THE PERSONALITY OF THE HOLY SPIRIT

The key to salvation, healing, deliverance, miracles and Christian living

JACOB IMONDU EDEHOMO

THE PERSONALITY OF THE HOLY SPIRIT

The key to salvation, healing, deliverance, miracles and Christian living

Copyright© 2018 Jacob Imondu Edehomo

Published in Nigeria by Jaya Publishers

Scripture quotations are from NEW KING JAMES VERSION of the Bibles unless otherwise indicated.

Dr. Jacob Imondu Edehomo
DOERS WORD OUTREACH
820 GROVE STREET,
IRVINGTON,NJ 07111- 3674

Email: eromodion1@yahoo.co.uk
        and favorchapel@gmail.com

cellphone +17173296321

ISBN 978-978-914-447-1

SECOND EDITION

DEDICATION

I dedicate this book, '*The Personality of the Holy Spirit*' to God Almighty through our Lord Jesus Christ by the power of the Holy Spirit and I pray that God's message about the good news of God's salvation, (healing, deliverance, spiritual welfare and Kingdom prosperity) be spread abroad by the power of the Holy Spirit to the utmost parts of the earth (Habakkuk 2:14).

ACKNOWLEDGMENT

Special thanks to my dear wife, Rev Mrs. Jayamma Alle, Fr. Rev. Robbie Prakasam, Evangelist Dansmith Aisevbo, the editors; Bishop Bernard Edehomo, Senior Pastor of the Divine Light Ambassadors Church (Ebenezer Chapel), Pastor Jude Samuel Ekpo, Senior Pastor of the Sanctuary of Kings Bible Church Nigeria and Mr. Kingsley Ehiemua, Department of Theatre Arts, Ambrose Alli University (AAU) Ekpoma

Thanks to Mrs Obehi Okoeki for typsetting the manuscript, Collins and Godspower Ugho and others friends and well-wishers who made this book a huge success, especially Pastor Felix Obhakhan of House of Levites Chapel Ekpoma and Pastor Akhere Ehiremen

FOREWORD

The book *"The Personality of the Holy Spirit"* is a must read for every one who desires to be excellent in life and in his or her area of calling. The first striking thing about this book is the title. One great misconception about the Holy Spirit **is His** personality. Many believers do not know that the Holy Spirit is a person. This book will give you a clear understanding of His person.

One crucial strength this book provides for every reader is the detailed knowledge of the Holy Spirit. This book in concise manner attempts to x-ray every issue bothering on the Holy Spirit. *The Personality of the Holy Spirit* seeks to help you gain mastery in the subject "The Holy Spirit".

Having been in ministry for more than twenty years, *The Personality of the Holy Spirit* excites me. My personal walk and experience with the Holy Spirit has been rewarding to my life and ministry. By the circle of God, I depend on the Holy Spirit for everything. Going through this book will help you arrive at this. This book promises you great experience and revival in the Holy Spirit.

In conclusion therefore, I have been privileged to author several books. I wish to commend the author for his style of writing this book. ***The Personality of the Holy Spirit*** *is* presented in such a way that every reader will be able to study, understand and apply to their life the Holy Spirit. The language is simple, concise and thought provoking.

God bless your soul. I greatly recommend this book for every believer.

Rev Emiowele Christopher
Founding pastor
Launch-Out into the Deep Ministries Inc.

CONTENT

PREFACE

This book about the Holy Spirit answers the fundamental questions which mankind has been attempting to understanding since the beginning of the world. Several people in the world do not know the person of the Holy Spirit. Even among believers the subject of the Holy Spirit has been a controversial one. Several people regard Him as an inanimate object, thereby sinning against Him...."*No one can say that Jesus Christ is Lord except by the Holy Spirit (1 Corinthian 12:3)*

As you read through this book prayerfully, you will find new meaning and genuine understanding of the Holy Spirit, the third divine person of the Godhead. This book will reveal the work of the Holy Spirit in creation, salvation, church ministry, proper realization of the great commission, as well as domestic activities as they affect the believers.

This book will help everyone who desires to know about the person of the Holy Spirit and His functions. This book is also very important to persons in other religions who wish to understand Jesus Christ and the power of His resurrection. This book deals with facts that stir the heart to its depth and awakens the emotions of the mind for proper understanding of the person of the Holy

Spirit. The style of the lessons is clearly expressed, easy to understand and the language is direct.

There are diversities of gifts, but the same Spirit, there are different ministries but the same God (1 Corinthians 12:4-5). The manifestation of the Spirit is given to each one for the profit of all: for to one is given the word of wisdom through the Spirit, to another the word of knowledge through the same Spirit, to another faith by the same Spirit, to another prophecy, to another discerning of spirits, to another different kinds of tongues, to another the interpretation of tongues (verses 7-10).

For by one spirit we were all baptized into one body whether Jews or Greeks, whether slaves or free and have all been made to drink into one spirit (verse 13). As many as are led by the spirit of God, they are the sons of God. When you receive the Holy Spirit, you will live a life free of fear, you will receive spiritual boldness (Romans 8:14-15). We are adopted as sons of God, so you are no more a slave if you have received the Holy Spirit into your heart. The Holy Spirit enables us to pray according to the will of God. He helps us when we are weak (Roman 8:26-27).

The Holy Spirit makes the church to live in harmony, in love with the avoidance of strife and rebellion. He brings unity; he does not encourage self-consciousness, but brings us to God-consciousness daily. He transforms you into an active, lively and functional human being. He destroys diseases and mortifies your sinful nature. Dare to ask for the wonderful gift of the Holy Spirit today and God will liberally give Him to you (Luke 11:9-13).

Under the Old Testament, people did not have the Holy Spirit as their comforter and He was not present to teach them all things as we are privileged to have Him today as our comforter. *"And look! The tears of the oppressed, but they have no comforter. On the side of their oppressors there is power. But they have no comforter"* *(Eccl. 4:1b)*

The new covenant is established on better promises; it is called the covenant of peace. The Old Testament brought no comfort to anyone, because the Holy Spirit had not come to stay permanently with God's children because Christ was not yet glorified. Only prophets, priests and kings had the Holy Spirit on them under the old covenant. What a privilege we have today! The average layman did not have access to the Holy Spirit in those days. *"When He, the spirit of truth is come He will guide you into all truth. He will show you things to come"*. (John 16:13,15).

The Holy Spirit is the spirit of truth whom Christ promised those who will believe the gospel. Nevertheless, our lord Jesus Christ said He was coming back to the world in the person of the Holy Spirit in order to comfort you. "I will not leave you comfortless. I will come to you" John 14:18. In verse 12-13. He said , verily, verily, I say unto you, he that believeth on me, the works that I do shall he do also; and greater works that these shall he do; because I go shall he also; and greater works than these shall he do; because I go unto my father and whatever, ye shall ask in my name, that will I do, that the father may be glorified in the son," (The King James study bible reference edition, edited by C.I. Scofield, pages 1135-1136).

Now Jesus Christ is glorified, all believers have received authority through the Holy Spirit over the devil and his demons in the name of Jesus Christ (Philippians 2:10-11). Our Lord Jesus Christ said, "Behold I give unto you power to tread upon serpent and scorpions, and over all the power of the enemy: and nothing shall be any means hurt you" (Luke 10:19). Now we have the Holy Spirit resident in us with the supernatural power of God. Hallelujah! Under this dispensation of grace, we have advantage of the Holy Spirit satanic manipulation and intimidations.

Because the Holy Spirit was not resident in the lives of the Israelites they had a great problem understanding the word of God, so many of them sinned against God and died in the wilderness. Moses interceded for them when God made up His mind to wipe them out and raise a nation out of Moses. But Moses refused the offer and instead reminded God of His promises to the nation of Israel. God repented and spared them (see Isaiah 59:9-15). The average Israelites in those days did not have any relationship with the Holy Spirit, so they perished without knowledge. "He that believeth on me, as the scripture hath said, out of his belly shall flow rivers of living water" (John 7:38-The King James study Bible Reference edition, edited by C.I. Scofield), page 1125. May the Lord bless you tremendously as you prayerfully read through this book in Jesus name!

CHAPTER ONE

PERSONALITY OF THE HOLY SPIRIT

The Old Testament scripture reading has gone a long way in explaining the doctrine of the Holy Spirit as follows:

1. The personality and deity of the Holy Spirit, attributes ascribed to Him, and His works.
2. He is revealed as sharing in the work of creation and therefore omnipotent, "… And the spirit of God was hovering over the face of waters" Genesis 1:2 (see also Psalm 104:30).

The Holy Spirit is revealed as omnipresent in Psalm 139:7-12, as striving with men in Genesis 6:3; as enlightener in Job 32:8 as one who gives us creative wisdom and skill in Exodus 28:3, 31:3. The Holy Spirit gives physical and spiritual strength (Judges 14:6, 19). He has executive and judicial ability and wisdom (Judges 3:10). He enables men to receive divine revelations (1 John 2:20).

The father has sent the Holy Spirit to indwell, guide, and empower believers (see Joel 2:28; John 16:13-15).

3. He is called God in Psalm 143:10; the spirit of judgment and burning in Isaiah 4:4; the spirit of the LORD, of wisdom of understanding, of counsel of might, of knowledge and of the fear of the LORD in Isaiah 11:2. He is the spirit of grace and supplications in Zechariah 12:10

4. In the dispensation of law under the Old Testament, the spirit acted in sovereignty, He came upon certain men and even upon a dumb donkey in Numbers 22-23. Now under the New Testament, anyone who believes in the Gospel and acts in faith receives the Holy Spirit freely. *"He who believes in Me, as the scripture has said, out of his heart will flow rivers of living water.*

But this He (Jesus) spoke concerning the Spirit, whom those believing in Him would receive for the Holy Spirit was not yet given, because Jesus was not yet glorified (John 7:38-39).

5. The Old Testament contains predictions of a future outpouring of the Spirit upon Israel (see Ezekiel 37:14; 39:29). And "upon all flesh" as predicted in the book of Joel 2:28, 29.

THE IMPORTANCE OF THE HOLY SPIRIT

a. The Holy Spirit is revealed as a divine third person of the Godhead (1 John 5:7) " For there are three that bear witness in heavens the father, the word and the Holy Spirit and these three are one" (see also, Mathew 28:19;2 Corinthians 13:14).

The Holy Spirit is not an errand boy as believed and thought by many people, rather He is equal with the father and the son. Take for instance, three brothers running a single company together (Edehomon & Co), their various names as John, Julius and Lucky, with John as the personal manager, Julius as the Production Manager and Lucky as the Sales Manager. These three person are one and owner of the same company. They are all managers, managing different departments of the company. These three people work together as one in order to achieve a common goal. So also, the Holy Spirit works in conjunction with the father and son in bringing mankind to kingdom of God and the father and son sent the Holy Spirit to be with us forever (John 14:16-26).

"And will pray the father, and He will give you another helper, that He may abide with you forever… But the helper, the Holy Spirit, whom the father will send in my name, He will teach you all things, and bring to your remembrance all things that I said to you" (see also, John 15:26; 16:7; Luke 24:49; Acts 2:33)

To understand the personality of the Holy Spirit you need to have a deeper insight of the trinity. The Holy Spirit is a living person because He can be approached, shunned, trusted, doubted, loved, hated, adored and insulted. The Holy Spirit is a divine person, Holy and equal to the father and son, therefore, we often practically acknowledge Him in praise, worship and benediction in every service and person devotion. We see the name of the Holy Spirit linked with the father and son in baptism. "o therefore and make disciples of all the nations baptizing them in the name of the father and of the son and of the Holy Spirit" (Mathew 28:19).

If you refer to Him as "it" (inanimate object), you need to repent and stop abusing Him. The Holy Spirit is a person and we must therefore address Him with the proper pronoun (He). "… He will testify of me" John 15:26.

"And when He has come, He will convict the world of sin.. He will guide you into all truth for he will not speak on His own authority but whatever He hears He will speak and He will tell you things to come. "He will glorify me, for He will take of what is mine and declare it to you.

Look out the following scripture verses in your Holy Bible John 6:7,8

"Nevertheless I tell you the truth. It is to you advantage that I go away; for if I do not go away the Helper will not come to you but if I depart I will send Him to come to you".

1. The Holy Spirit preaches Jesus (Acts 5:32)

2. He reproved and convicts us of sin, judgement and righteousness.
3. He guides us into all truth about God's kingdom.
4. He speaks in the authority of Christ.
5. He says whatever He hears from Christ.
6. He tells us things to come.
7. He glorifies Jesus in every thing.
8. He reveals the mind of Christ to us.

With the help of the Holy Spirit, we have come to understand that Jesus Christ came to die not only for the Jews, but also for the entire world.

"For God so loves the world that He gave His only begotten son, that whosoever believes in Him should not perish but have everlasting life" (John 3:16, 1 John 2:2).

"And He himself is the propitiation for our sins, and not for ours only but also for the whole world" (1 John 2:2)

He convicts us to our sin of unbelief, which is the basis of all sins that lead to death. Mark 16:16 states. "He who believes and is baptized will be saved; but he who does not believe will be condemned".

Luke, 8:13 states: "But the ones on the rock are those who when they hear, receive the word with joy; and these have no root, who believe for a while and time of temptation fall away. "See John, 3:16-20,36;5:24,38,8:24;10:26).

This is the reason why when any true servant of God preaches or shares the good news under the direction of the Holy Spirit, it convicts us (both believers and unbelievers) of our sins. The Holy Ghost revealed the mind of Christ to us by convicting men to repent and be saved from the coming wrath and judgment. Often many marvel and say "who told the man of God about my secret (subtle) sins unknown to man? But the Holy Ghost does. A sensible person, who is convicted of his or her wrong doing by the Holy Spirit, comes quickly to repentance, but the hardened in mind dies without knowledge, they shun His conviction and fail to repent.

We have seen many armed robbers, prostitutes, adulterers, cultists, liars, fornicator, assassins, covetous idolaters and evil perpetrators repenting after listening to a sermon preached through the demonstration of the Holy Spirit. In conviction they repented and got saved, but the one with unbelief in his or her heart died in their sins and go to hell fire. Jesus wishes to see all men saved through sincere repentance. The Holy Spirit is the spirit of truth (John 16:13, 15).

The Holy Spirit makes us to understand that self-righteousness is vain (Isaiah 64:6) "But we are all like an unclean thing. And all our righteousness are like filthy rags…"

"For they being ignorant of God's righteousness and seeking to establish their own righteousness, have not submitted to the righteousness of God" (Roman 10:3).

The righteousness of Christ is what we need 1 Corinthians 1:30-31 states: "But of Him you are in Christ Jesus, who becomes for us wisdom from and righteousness and sanctification and redemption- that as it written, He who glories, let him glory in the LORD".

It is only through Him alone by faith that we can become righteous (see Roman 3:22, 25; 2 Corinthians 5:14, 21). Jesus said in John 14:12 that those people who believe in His word shall do greater works through the indwelling of the Holy Spirit. True to the word of Christ today, many which have received the Holy Spirit into their hearts do great works of miracles, signs and wonders all over the world. Our Lord Jesus Christ is there in heaven sitting at the right hand of the father as our intercessor, and the power of God is indwelling His church through the help of the Holy Spirit; he enlightens all people who believe in Christ..

The Holy Spirit speaks to our ears, like when He spoke Cornelius to send men to Joppa and call Simon in Acts. 10:32. "Send therefore to Joppa and call Simon here, whose surname is Peter. He is lodging in the house of Simon, a Tanner, by the sea. When He comes, he will speak to you".

The Holy Spirit knows everything, number, name, street and places. We must stop underrating Him, His personality and His ministry especially when He speaks through His servants.

1. He is the one who makes us to be born again. John 3:3,5
2. He is a life giver. (John 6:63; Roman 8:11).
3. The Holy Spirit impacts us with power (John 7:37-39, 14:12-17; Luke 24:49; Acts 1:4-8, 10:38).
4. The Holy Spirit is our comforter. The Greek word "Parakletos" means "one alongside". He is a personal companion. A helper, (see John 14:16, 26; 15:26).
5. The Holy Spirit is our teacher, teacher of truth (John 14:17; 26;15:26;16:13).
6. The Holy Spirit reminds us of all truth (John 14:26).
7. The Holy Spirit guides us into all truth (John 16:13).
8. The Holy Spirit reveal Christ to people (John 16:13-15)

9. The Holy Spirit reveals events (John 16:13)
10. The Holy Spirit is a glorifier of Christ (John 16:14)
11. The Holy Spirit is a chief witness for Christ (John 15:26; 16:13 15; Acts 1:8)
12. The Holy Spirit convinces sinners of sin, righteousness and judgement (John 16:8) as I have previously pointed out.

b.   The revelation concerning the Holy Spirit.

This revelation is however, very progressive in NT (New Testament) than in OT (Old Testament), for instance, during the earthly ministry of our Lord Jesus Christ. He taught His disciples in Luke 9:13 that they shall receive the Spirit through prayer to the father. He promised that He would Himself pray to the father to send them the Holy Spirit and in answer to His prayer, the Holy Spirit came to the disciples in the upper room where they were assembled in obedience to the command of Christ (Acts 2:1-5). Before then, Christ breathed on them saying: "Receive ye the Holy Ghost" (John 20:22). The King James Reference Edition Edited by C.I. Scofield page 1144. It was after that first experience that he instructed them to wait in Jerusalem for a second experience that would give them power when the Holy Spirit come upon them to enable them fulfill their ministry (see Luke 24:49: Acts 1:8).

On the day of Pentecost , the spirit came upon the whole body of believers (Acts 2:1-4). After Pentecost, the gospel was preached to the Jews, and the spirit was impacted to such as believed by the laying on of hands (Acts 8:14-17).

Apostle Peter opened the door of the Kingdom to the Gentiles (Acts 10). Through the help of the Holy Spirit faith was given to those who believed (Acts 10:44; 11:15,18), this remained the permanent mark for the entire church-age.

The Holy Spirit will come upon all who believe. See Mark 16:17-18: "And these signs will follow those who believe: in my name they will cast out demons; they will speak with new tongues; they will take up serpents; and if they drink anything deadly, it will by no means hurt them; they will lay hands on the sick, and they will recover".

You only need faith to activate this, else you will not be able to function as a believer or a pastor/evangelist. If you lack the power of the Holy Spirit, the powers of darkness will grind you to dust. But if you have faith to believe and activate the Holy Spirit in you, you shall live a victorious Christian life, in absolute dominion over the forces of wickedness.

Many believers and even pastors do not function in this capacity because they do not have faith to activate the power of the Holy Spirit that is in them. So, the devil still torments them and gets them killed because they have lost dominion to Satan in fear and unbelief.

Note: Every believer is born of the Spirit (John 3:3, 6; 1 John 5:1) by the spirit the believers are brought into one body and baptized by the same spirit (1 Corinthians 12:12, 13, 1 John 2:27), thus sealing him for God (Ephesians 1:13, 4:30).

c.   The Holy Spirit is the believers' privilege and right to the inheritance of God through Christ. (Acts 2:4; 4:29-31, Ephesians 1:13, 14, 18).

There is a difference between baptism and indwelling of the Holy Spirit. While baptism of the first experience that brings and unites a believers with the body of Christ, indwelling is the second experience that brings the power of God into the life of the believer for the works of the ministry.

d.   The Holy Spirit is related to Christ:

In His conception (Mathew 1:18, 20; Luke 1:35), in baptism (Mathew 3:16, Mark 1:10, John 1:32, 33), In the works of service (Luke 4:1,14, Acts 10:38), at resurrection (Romans 8:11) and as His witness throughout this age (John 16:8, 11,13,14).

e.   The Holy Spirit forms the true church: (Mathew 16:18, 1 Corinthians 12:13, 27) "And I also say to you that you are Peter, and on this rock, I will build my church and the gates of Hades shall not prevail against it."

He baptizes all believers into the body of Christ (1 Corinthians 12:12, 13). "For as the body is one and has many members, but all the members of that one body, being many, are one body, so also is Christ.

"For by one Spirit we were all baptized into one body-whether Jews or Greeks whether slaves or free- and have all been made to drink into one spirit.

He impacts gifts for service to every member of the body of Christ (1 Corinthians 12:77-11, 28-30). But unfortunately, many of us use the gifts for wrong purposes even in serving idols, like the stiff-necked Israelites did, after God has rescued them from long slavery in Egypt. They created a golden calf and worshipped it, just like many do today.

He guides members of the body of Christ in service unto God (Luke 2:25-27; 4:1;Acts 16:6-10) and He empowers them for service (Acts 1:18; 2:1-4; 1 Corinthians 2:4).'

f.   The spirit abides in company of believers: The company of believers constitutes the local church and He makes of them a corporate temple (1 Corinthians 3:16, 17).

G.   A threefold personal relationship: Christ indicates a threefold personal relationship of the Spirit to the believer "with", "in" "upon" (John 141:17; Luke 24:19; Acts 1:8) "which "indicates the approach of God to the souls. Convicting them of sin (John 16:9) by presenting Christ as the object of faith (John 16:14) imparting faith (Ephesians 2:8) and regeneration (John 3:3, 16) "in" describes the abiding presence of the Spirit of believers (1 Corinthian 6:19) to give believers victory over the flesh (Romans 8:2, 4 Galatians 5:16, 17).

The Holy Spirit creates the Christian character (Galatians 5:22, 23). And helps our infirmities (Romans 8:26-27). He helps us to realize that we are the sons of God (Galatians 4:6) he enables us to apply the scriptures for cleansing and sanctification. (Ephesians 5:26; 2 Thessalonians 2:13, 1 Peter 1:2). The Holy Spirit comfort us and intercedes for believers (Acts 9:31; Romans 8:26-27), and reveals the mind of Christ (John 16:14).

H. **He can be grieved:** Unbelievers & believers who blaspheme the spirit of God commit sins against the Holy Spirit (Mathew 12:31).

Therefore I say to you, every sin and blasphemy will be forgiven men, but the blasphemy against the spirit will not be forgiven men! (Mathew 12:31).

He can be resisted and insulted (Hebrews 3:7-19). The Holy Spirit is very important in the life of believers, but believers usually commit sin against Him when they grieve Him by allowing evil in their heart of life (Ephesians 4:30, 31) or quench Him by disobedience (1 Thessalonians 5:19). As believers we must put away every attitude or action that may likely hinder His power and be ready at all times to yield to His leading in works of service constantly, so as to make progress in our calling and ministry in Jesus name Amen.

The symbols of the Holy Spirit

1. Oil (Hebrews 1:9)
2. Water (John 7:38,39)
3. Wind (Acts 2:2; John 3:8)
4. Fire (Acts 2:3)
5. A dove (Mathew 3:16)
6. A seal Ephesians 1:13-14

CHAPTER TWO
DEITY OF THE HOLY SPIRIT

Since we now aware that the Holy Spirit is a Divine Person, though He does not posses a human body like ours. The Holy Spirit is God Almighty, as the scripture makes certain strong statements in that passage of the Bible. "…Satan filled your Heart to lie to the Holy Spirit… you have not lied to men but God" (Acts 5:3,4).

Ananias and Saphira who vowed to give some amount of money to the church from the sales of his land, got carried away by flesh and lied to the Holy Ghost who is also God and they were punished by death. The Holy Spirit has equal divine attributes with the father and son in all respects.

The Holy Spirit is joined with the father and son in the process of baptism as one and the same "… in the name of the FATHER and of the SON and of the HOLY SPIRIT" (Mathew 28:19). Also in the church benediction: "…the grace of the Lord Jesus Christ, and the love of God and the communion of the HOLY SPIRIT, be with you all" (2 Corinthians 13:14).

The Holy Spirit is eternal (Hebrew 9:14) "how much more, will the blood of Christ, who through the eternal offered Himself unblemished to God, cleanse our consciences from acts that lead to death, so that we may serve the living God (The NIV Tropical Study Bible) page 1374.

The Holy Spirit is omnipotent (Luke 1:35) "The Holy Spirit will come upon you, and the power of the Most High will overshadow you. So the Holy one to be born will be called the son of God." The Holy Spirit is the power behind creation see (Gen 1:2).

The Holy Spirit is omniscient (1 Corinthians 2:10, 11). The spirit of God searches all things the Holy Spirit is intelligent, so He is our instructor (see Nehemiah 9:20) "you also gave your good spirit to instruct them, and did not withhold your manna from their mouth, and give them water for their thirst".

He is knowledgeable (Romans 8:27, 1 Corinthians 2:10, 12). Knows things, He has will power (1 Corinthians 12:11)

'But one and the same spirit works all these things distributing such one individually as He wills".

He can make decision and as well teach. See John 14:26 and guides us (John 16:12, 13). He helps ministers and individuals who are obedient to Him.

Under the Old Testament during the cure of Naaman's leprosy by Elisha the servant of the Lord in 2 Kings 5:25, 27, Gehazi lied to the Holy Spirit who is full of knowledge, similar to the case of Ananias and Sapphira, so, he was punished with generational leprosy. The same thing still happens in most of our churches today. As a result, many servants of God and believers have their lives terminated, since they are taking the office of the Holy Spirit for granted. He watches the secret affairs of man and searches the deep things of God and man. Also he helps true believers to discern people spiritually by x-raying the behavior and acts of men.

The Holy Spirit is omnipresent: "where can I go from your spirit? Where can I flee from your presence? If I go up to the heavens wings of the dawn, If I settle on the far side of the sea even there you hand will guide, your right hand will hold fast" (Psalm 139:7, 10) (NIV). **The Holy Spirit is present everywhere is the reason why distance is never a barrier to the healing power of our LORD.**

The Holy Spirit is the power network that transmits our prayer through Jesus Christ to God in acting unity. We have seen in a number of times people rescued from a collapsed building after three months of the incident. Even those who accidentally fall into the toilet and pits are picked up alive through the power of the Holy Spirit and in the recent years, Tsunami, Haiti disaster is a typical example that it is only God through the Holy Spirit that can control weather and preserve souls. The Holy Spirit is present in all places and in three places (heaven, earth and beneath the earth).

The Holy Spirit is an Author: The author of the sixty-six chapters of the Holy Bible is the Holy Spirit; the pages of the bible are authoritative revelations in written form of God's nature and purpose as the Holy Spirit dictate to the inspired authors over a period of 1600 years by these different types of people in different parts of the world, without dispute or controversy. The best proofs of His divine inspiration for so many different men to write book without contradiction is a miracle which can only be explained by the Author's guiding hand.

John Calvin said, "God had dictated the scripture". Through the power of the Holy Spirit's utterance supplied by God, it was communicated, inspired and impacted to holy men of God. Example is Moses in Exodus 19 and 20; God spoke through Moses is giving him the world and commandment of God for His people Israel.

HOLINESS: The spirit of God is holy and pure. The world 'holy' is an adjectives describing God's sprit as decent, sinless and pure in all ramifications, likewise, every child of God must possess the same attributes as the Holy Spirit, willing to be free from all deceit. "But as He who called you is holy, you also be holy in all your conduct, because it is written, be holy, for I am holy" (1 Peter 1:15-16).

Nehemiah 9:20 makes us to understand that He is benevolent the Holy Spirit acting in unity with God the father could do things God Himself does in the following categories below:

Creation (Job 33:4)

Salvation (1 Corinthians 6:11)

Giving life (John 6:63)

Speaking in prophecy (2 Peter 1:21) notify us of His coming wrath (John 16:8,11).

The Holy Spirit as an entity: Many people get lost and find it difficult to understand that the Holy Spirit is a separate person acting in union with God the father and the son. This could easily be reconciled by the baptismal formula in the great commission in Mathew 28:19 as well as baptism of our LORD JESUS in the book of Luke 3:21, 22.

"Go therefore and make disciples of all the nations, baptizing them in the name of the father and of the son and of the Holy Spirit" (Mathew 28:19).

Luke 3:21-22 says "…And while He prayed the heaven was opened and the Holy Spirit descended in bodily form like a dove upon Him, and a voice came from heaven which said, "You are my beloved son; in you I am well pleased".

We have clearly seen the evidence that God the Father, Son and the Holy Spirit are the same. "You are my beloved son; in you I am well pleased" John baptized God the son in River Jordan and God the Holy spirit alighted on our LORD like a dove, one of the symbols of the Holy Spirit and God the father confirmed the son by His spoken word from heaven. We can also see that God is a triune being, body soul and spirit as we are (see 1 Thessalonians 5:23).

The Holy Spirit united with God the father and the son was sent to the earth to be with the believers till Jesus return in glory for the harvest of the saints and He obey the command.

"But the helper, the Holy Spirit, whom the father will send in my name, he will teach you all thing to your remembrance all things that I said to you" (Joh 14:26).

The son (JESUS CHRIST) in His love, promised to send the Holy Spirit to the church (believers)

The church (believers) must follow the leading/prompting of the Holy Spirit as a director of the mission of our Lord Jesus Christ ; a good example was Paul's mission to Macedonia in Acts 16:6-7.

"Now when they had gone through Phrygia and the region of Galatia, there were forbidden by the Holy Spirit to preach the word in Asia. After they had come to Mysia, they tried to go into Bithynia but the spirit did not permit them" (Acts, 16:6-7).

As a pastor, evangelist, prophet or believer, you must adhere strictly to the leading of the Holy Spirit in carrying out God's task, doing things your own way could be regarded as insubordination, and you may be liable to destruction and hell fire like Balaam, Ananias and Sapphira, and Judas Iscariot etc.

He was referred to as the Spirit in NKJV in verse 7 but the spirit did not permit them; while NIV said "The spirit of JESUS "And the King James, study Reference Edition by Scofield put it as "The Holy Ghost". He is called "the spirit of God". In Romans 8:9 The Holy Spirit in collaboration with the father and son speaks not of Himself but always says what is dictated to Him (see scripture proof in John (16:13)".... For He will not speak on His own authority and whatever he hears He will speak; and He will tell you things to come".

The Holy Spirit glorifies Christ (John 16:14).

CHAPTER THREE
THE WORK OF THE HOLY SPIRIT IN THE WORLD

INTRODUCTION: The activities of the Holy Spirit in the world since creation till Pentecost cannot be over emphasized. His activities revolve around the following: the preservation of the universe in relation to the unbelievers, the writing of the Holy Scriptures, conception of the Lord Jesus Christ and His ministry, and domestic life of spirit filled believers and children of GOD in general.

The only difference between the dispensation of grace and of law is that the Holy Spirit was never permanent in the Old Testament unlike the New Testament where He is permanently living with us as believers. "And I will pray the Father, and He will give you another helper, that he may abide with you forever". (John 14:16).

During the Old Testament He was on a come and go affairs, this was why David prayed in Psalm 51:11, saying: "... do not take your Holy Spirit from me". But today, the Holy Spirit has come to stay permanently; therefore, this kind of prayers is no more valid. The Holy Spirit has come to indwell believers with a receptive heart in this dispensation of grace.

The Holy Spirit came upon Jephthah in Judges 11:29 and he became valiant. Also, David received the Holy Spirit on him when Samuel anointed him with a horn of oil and he became valiant. But when Saul committed a sin against God, the Holy Spirit departed from Saul and an evil spirit tormented him. See Samuel 16:13-14, 1 Samuel 15:24-29. Saul also committed the sin of Necromancy

(see 1 Samuel 28:6,25) the   Holy Spirit left Saul because of all these sins.

"But the Spirit of the Lord departed from Saul, and a distressing spirit from the LORD troubled him". (1 Samuel 16:14).

At that time the Holy Spirit had not yet started indwelling in human beings, so, He departed from him. But the New Testament the case is different. "For the gifts and the calling of God are irrevocable" (Romans 11:29).

All it requires for the Holy Spirit continues with you forever is repentance from your wrong doings (Read verses 30, 36)

THE HOLY SPIRIT IN CREATION'

Genesis 1:2 reveals to us that the Holy Spirit was an active personality during the creation of the world". And the Spirit of GOD was hovering over the surface of the waters".

"By faith we understand that the worlds were framed by the word of God, so that the things which are seen were made of things which are visible" (Hebrew 11:3). "By the word of the

LORD the heavens were made and all the host of them by the breath of His mouth" (Psalm 33:6).

By the Holy Spirit things were created by God and kept alive, just as man was created a tripartite being and preserved alive (see 1 Thessalonians 5:23) Man is a triune being body, soul and spirit. If the Holy Spirit is absent in man he becomes carnally minded, and it amounts to death (Rom 8:5-8).

THE HOLY SPIRIT IN THE PRESERVATION OF THE UNIVERSE

The Holy Spirit creates and preserves the grass and us likewise and He is also capable of destroying it at will. By the word of God and the power of the Holy Spirit, the universe is renewed (Psalm 104:30). "Until the spirit is poured upon us from on high and the wilderness becomes a fruitful field, and the fruitful field is counted as a forest" (Isaiah 32:15). Also see Isaiah 40:7.

THE HOLY SPIRIT TO THE UNBELIEVERS

The Holy Spirit as a cleansing agent has come to reprove the world of sin, righteousness and judgment. The Holy Spirit operates in the conscience of men through the word of God, convincing them of sin, for His word is a edged sword (Hebrew 4:12) that convicts men of their sins (John 16:8, 11).

THE HOLY SPIRIT IN RELATION TO SCIPTURES

The Holy bible tells us that the Holy Spirit is the author of the scripture in the book of 2 Peter 1:20, 21 as well as the interpreter of the scriptures to us (John 16:14, 14:26). "He will glorify me, for He will take of what is mine and declare it to you" (John 16:14).

"Knowing this first, that no prophecy of the scripture is of any private interpretation, for prophecy never came by the will of man, but holy men of God spoke as they were moved by the Holy Spirit (2 Peter 1, 20, 21).

The scripture aids believers in evangelism/outreaches especially when sharing sermon among the congregation of believers atheist, skeptic and heckler, false teachers and prophets that propagate heresies with backsliding souls, He takes us to in depth knowledge about the word of God and enables us to dismantle all false arguments. Personally, the Holy Spirit has helped me a lot and He is still helping me till now, enabling me to carry out great commission as a witness of Christ and as a pastor.

One faithful day in Tripoli, Libya North Africa Bro. Martins Duru of blessed memory and I went to witness Christ to one brother Barnabas, He asked hard question from the scriptures but to God be the Glory I answered him as Holy Spirit reminded and directed. Brother Barnabas had a warm handshake with me, for the Holy Ghost gave me right interpretation and he was satisfied.

THE HOLY SPIRIT IN RELATION TO JESUS CHRIST

The Holy Spirit in bodily form concieved our LORD JESUS CHRIST. See Luke 1:35. And he became of age, He was led by the Holy Spirit into the wilderness to be tested (Mathew 4:1).

The Holy Spirit anointed Jesus Christ our Lord (1 John 2:20, 27) and commissioned Him for service.

"How God anointed Jesus of Nazareth with the Holy Spirit and with power who went about doing good and healing all who were oppressed by the devil, for God was with Him" (Acts 10:38).

The Holy Spirit personally anointed me for service, I was a novice in the word and I found myself automatically speaking scriptures.

Through the power of the Holy Spirit, Jesus was crucified (Hebrew 9:14) and He was resurrected from the grave by the same power of the Holy Spirit (Rom 8:11).

Jesus Christ was teaching His disciples and the church through the Holy Spirit and He gave His Apostles commandment through the Holy Spirit (Acts 1:2).

The promise of the Holy Spirit was given to the believers. "Therefore being exalted to the right hand of God, and having received from the father the promise of the Holy Spirit, He poured out this which you now see and hear" (Acts 2:33).

The Holy Spirit empowered and qualified the Messiah for His official task and enabled Him to destroy the kingdom of Satan and He established the Kingdom of God by the Spirit. Jesus Christ cast out demons by the Holy Spirit (Mathew 12:28.)

CHAPTER FOUR
THE WORK OF THE HOLY SPIRIT IN THE MINISTRY OF CHRIST

CHRIST CONCEVIED

The ministry of the Holy Spirit was made manifest in the New Testament powerfully starting from the conception of Christ.

"…And the Angel answered and said to her, the Holy Spirit will come upon you and the power of the highest will over shadow you; therefore also, that Holy One who is to be born will be called the son of God" (Luke 1:35).

And the Angle of the LORD informed Mary in verse 36 that her relative Elizabeth has also conceived a son in her old age after she had been called barren.

Mary believed and said … "For with God nothing will be impossible" (verse 37).

When Mary again was in the house of Zechariah to greet her sister Elizabeth, the Holy Spirit manifested Himself.

"And it happened when Elizabeth heard the greetings of Mary, that the babe leaped in her womb: and Elizabeth was filled with the Holy Spirit.

Then He spoke out with a loud voice and said, "Blessed are you among women, and blessed is the fruit of your womb! But why is this granted to me, that the mother of my LORD should come to me? For indeed as soon as the voice of your greeting sounded in my ears, the babe leaped in my womb for joy" (Luke 1:41-44).

At the state of conception, Mary felt a great Joy that she could be so honored by God to be the one to conceive and give birth to the savior of the whole world, so she exclaimed!.

"...My soul magnifies the Lord and my spirit has rejoiced in God my savior. For He has regarded the lonely state of His maidservant, for behold, henceforth all generations will call me blessed. For he who is mighty has done great things for me, and the Holy is His name and His mercy is on those who fear Him from generation to generation" (Luke 1:46-50.)

Jesus Christ was born in Bethlehem, and He grew and became strong in the spirit, and was in the desert till the day of His manifestation of Israel.

MIRACLE PERFORMED

Jesus Christ performed a lot of miracles with help of the Holy Spirit as revealed in the Gospel.

"But if I cast out demons by the Spirit of God, surely the Kingdom of God has come upon you" (Mathew 12:28).

The Holy Spirit is the greatest warrior in heaven, earth and beneath, he can destroy any giant that strives with God's elect or people. We see from Christ's ministry how He used the power to dismantle sickness, diseases and afflictions that were placed on people by the devil.

ANOINTED

The Holy Spirit anointed Jesus after his baptism by John in River Jordan, prior to when He was led to the wilderness to be tempted by Satan. Mathew 3:16 *"when He had been baptized, Jesus came up immediately from the water, and behold the heavens were opened to Him, and He saw the Spirit of God descending like a dove and alighting upon Him. And suddenly a voice came from heaven, saying, this is my beloved son in whom I am well pleased"*.

SUPPORTED BY THE HOLY SPIRIT

The Holy Spirit was always supporting Jesus Christ since the day he was filled by the Holy Spirit at Jordan, He returned from Jordan and was led by the Spirit into the wilderness" (Luke 4:1)

"And He was handed the book of the prophet Isaiah. And when He had opened the book, he found the place where it was written. The spirit of the Lord is upon me, because He has anointed me to preach the gospel to the poor; He has sent me to heal the broken hearted, to proclaim liberty to the captives and recovery of sight to the blind; to set at liberty those who are oppressed; to proclaim the acceptable year of the Lord" (verses 17-18).

Jesus was filled with the Holy Spirit and enabled to do the work of the kingdom.

"… Jesus being filled with the Holy Spirit, returned from Jordan, and was led by the Spirit into the wilderness" (Luke 4:1)

Through the eternal spirit, Jesus Christ offered Himself to God without spot, cleansed our conscience from dead works to serve the living God (Hebrew 9:14) He was also raised by the power of the Holy Spirit from death. Jesus Christ through the power of the Holy Spirit was justified.

"And without controversy great is the mystery of Godliness. God was manifested in the flesh, justified in the Spirit, seen by angles, preached among the Gentiles, believed on it the world, received up in glory" (1 Timothy 3:16)

CHAPTER FIVE
THE MINISTRY OF THE HOLY SPIRIT IN THE CHURCH

When a church is filled with the Holy Spirit, it a sign and evidence that such a church of God. Every member of such a church will be seen living according to God's word and bearing the fruit of the Holy Spirit.

The Holy Spirit appeals to believers in the name of our Lord Jesus Christ, that all should agree with one another so that there may be no division among believers and that all may be perfected and united in mind and thoughts. Any church that is filled with orgies and drunkenness, sexual immorality and debauchery, dissension and jealously rather than clothing themselves with the Lord Jesus Christ and free from gratifying the desire of the sinful nature as in Galatians 5:19, 21, lacks the power of the Holy Spirit. We are expected to put on spiritual clothing of Christ (Galatians 3:27; Zechariah 3:4).

Since the Holy Spirit baptizes all the church members into the body of Christ, they have become the offspring of God-brothers and sisters, relative of the same parents. They are to live as family members by the overlooking social differences, forgiving each other, not judging or destroying each other and above all loving one another.

Romans 12:10- "Be kindly affectionate to one another with brotherly love, in honor giving preference to one another.".

Another sign of living church is the indwelling of the Holy Spirit, speaking with other tongues.

"And they were filled with the Holy Spirit and began to speak with other tongues as the spirit gave them utterance" (Acts 2:4).

When I became a Christian in my third year at the Federal Polytechnic Oko, Anambra State, during my Higher National Diploma, speaking with other tongue was a strange thing to me then. In fact, I condemned those who speak in tongues then ignorantly thinking they were insane. I was yet to speak in tongues then, being an ardent Roman Catholic, baptized and confirmed at Mary the Queen Catholic Church, Ekpoma, Edo State Nigeria. Suddenly a good friend of mine Ofonime Umoren, nicknamed U.K. introduced me to the Chapel of Transfiguration at the Polytechnic premises, a non-denominational church. Gradually, as I listed to the word of the Lord and the advice of my friend Ofonime, I stopped smoking, drinking and fornicating with girls on campus. I became sharpened with the salvation message from that church. Because of this, during my National Youth Service, 1999, with News and Current Affairs Ebonyi Broadcasting Service (EBBS) Abakaliki, Ebonyi State, Nigeria, I had an opportunity to become a member of the Nigeria Christian Corpers Fellowship (NCCF) which again lifted my spirit and enabled me to know Christ more. In the year 2000, the month of September, I left Nigeria for North Africa (Tripoli).

Then, the Lord Jesus Christ commissioned me. I had an opportunity to serve in two ministries, first in the ministry of Evangelist Dansmith Aisevbho, Deliverance/Healing Ministry, during his twelve year stay in Libya. When Evangelist Dansmith left Tripoli for Nigeria, then I served under the ministry of Reverend Fr. Robbie Prakasam of the church of Christ the King (Anglican Communion) for another year as an Evangelist, church coordinator and Elder. My Reverend Father Robbie had ever loved me and kept telling me more of speaking with new tongues. He encouraged me to ask God for the gift of speaking in tongues.

I remember he hold me that it is a language that the devil cannot discern. He speaks more of tongues and do share his testimony with me of how in one of the orthodox seminaries, he was to be rejected, but God later intervened and he was ordained priest in the Anglican Communion. Father Robbie speaks more in tongues and prophesies a lot, a lovely gentleman about 65 years of age, then, an experienced priest. I loved living with him. As a church Elder and coordinator, he always laid his hands on me prophesying upon my life and he prayed for me for the gift of speaking in tongues.

December 2004, I was divinely instructed by the Lord through the Holy Spirit, while I was sitting at the Garden along Qammar Mufftah Road, to go to Nigeria and witness to my family because, I was raised from the family of Idolatry like father Abraham.

Immediately I arrived in Nigeria I met my brother the Senior Pastor of Divine Light Ambassadors Church (DLAC) (Favor Chapel) Lagos, Nigeria and requested of Him to be baptized by total immersion, since after I left Roman Catholic I never had it. After the exercise in one of the rivers in Lagos, I began to speak in tongues. Now I blast in Tongues as If I am blowing a trumpet what a lovely experience encountered. Apostle Paul said he thanks God he speaks in tongues than everyone, in 1 Corinthians 14:21, 25. "With men of other tongues and other lips I will speak to this people, and yet, for all that they will not hear me says the Lord.

Therefore, tongues are for a sign, not to those who believe, but to unbelievers, but prophecy is not for unbelievers but for those who believe.

Speaking in tongues in church is for the edification of the body of Christ (verse 26). It is of course very vital. When we speak in other tongues, the devil is confused.

Song:
Amen, Amen
We bind the devil,
We loose Gods power in this place
We speak in tongues
Satan is confused
Deliverance follows
Amen!

Tongues are a spiritual heavenly language. When you speak in tongues, you speak mysteries that are unknown to Satan and his cohorts. So whenever you start speaking it, it edifies you and brings you to spiritual stability.

In one of our local churches where I had previously pastured for 15 years, at Divine Light Ambassadors Church (Ebenezer Chapel), Ekpoma parish, every second Friday of the Month, 11pm-4.30am, Nigerian time, is our "Purpose Night" (Vigil) This service ushers us into the new month with the blessing of God.

On one faithful Friday night of such fellowship, 24th June 2005 we shared and meditated on "playing with Fire" "The snare of witchcraft and occultism", and "why do you want to die?" (Deuteronomy 18:9-14).

Before I started my meditation on the above scripture readings I spoke in an unknown tongue for a very long time as the spirit enabled me.

After the "Purpose Night" a woman in our church who is about 65 years old who was absent at the vigil came to meet me at the church on Saturday morning and started narrating how she was rescued the previous night from witchcraft attack and demonic attack. She narrated that they came chasing her in the dream with cutlass, but suddenly she spoke in tongues and immediately the pursuers (witches) made a u-turn and ran away and she was saved. The moment she narrated her experienced to me, I caught the revelation. And the next Sunday service 26th June 2005; she also shared an open testimony at the church service. Since that day no witch or demon has ever come to her again. And she is now a committed member of the church. As a matter of fact, I thank God for this testimony in the church.

And they overcame by the blood of the lamb and by the word of their testimony..." (Revelation 12:11)

In addition, when we speak in other tongues in the church, let us try and pray for the gift of interpretation too, because he who speaks in an unknown tongue edifies himself, but he who prophesies edifies the church. The scripture further says:

"He who speaks in a tongue edifies himself, but he who prophesied edifies the church. I wish you all spoke with tongues, but even more that you prophesied: for he who prophecies is greater than he who speaks with tongues: unless indeed he interprets, that the church may receive edification.

But now, brethren, if I came to you speaking with tongues, what shall I profit you unless I speak to you either by revelation by knowledge by prophesying, or by teaching? Even things without life, whether flute or harp. When they make a sound, unless they make a distinction in the sounds, how will it be known what is piped or played? For if the trumpet makes an uncertain sound, unless they make a distinction in the sounds, how will it be known what is piped or played? For if the trumpet makes an uncertain sound, who will prepare for battle? So likewise you, unless you utter by the tongue words easy to understand, how will it be known what is spoken? For you will be speaking into the air…even so you, since you are zealous for spiritual gifts, let it be for the edification of the church that you seek to excel. Therefore let him who speaks in a tongue pray that he may interpret". (1 Corinthians 14:4-9, 12-13).

BAPTIZES: The Holy Spirit baptizes the body of Christ.

"For by one Spirit we were all baptized into one body – whether
Jews or Greeks, whether slave or free and have all been made to drinks into one spirit: (1 Corinthians 12:13)

The same spirit brings about the fellowship person to person contact between Christian, sharing their hearts' feelings living together and giving to one another from that which God has given them others (building Spiritual unity among believers).

"…I indeed baptize you with water: but one mightier than I is coming, whose sandal strap I am not worthy loose. He will baptize you with the Holy spirit and fire". Luke 3:16.

See the conversion and baptism of Cornelius and his household in Acts 10: 34, 48.

When they heard all these things they became silent: and they glorified God saying, then God has also granted to the gentiles repentance to life." Acts 11:18.

So God who knows the heart acknowledged them and giving them the Holy Spirit just as He did to us. And made no distinction between us and them, purifying their heart by faith." Acts 15:8-9

In addition, see also the conversation of Lydia in Acts 16:13-15 and the jailer in Acts 16:25-34. The conversation of Lydia brought the goodness of God to Europe, as well as the conversion of the household of the jailer, the Holy Spirit converted his household to God.

The baptism of Lydia's household in a building was not specified, as tradition proves that infants and all were baptized, I don't think children were baptized because the word **"Baptized"** is offered in Greek as *:"baptizo"*, meaning to dip or immense completely. It symbolizes the identification of a believer with the death, burial and resurrection of our Lord Jesus Christ.

Also see the conversation of the Corinthians. "Then Crispus, the ruler of the synagogue believed on the Lord with all his household. And many of the Corinthians, hearing and were baptized" (Acts 18:8).

In Ephesus, Paul's preaching caused a riot because the power of God moved and many got baptized as he laid hands on them.

"And when Paul had laid hands on them, the Holy Spirit came upon them, and they spoke with tongues and prophesied" (Acts 19:1-5). The conversation of Paul in Acts 9:1,8 and Acts 22:1,6 is exceptional.

"...Brother Saul, the Lord Jesus who appeared to you on the road as you came has sent me that you may receive your sight and be filled with the Holy Spirit". Acts. 9:17

Immediately there fell from his eyes something like scales and he received his sight at once: and he arose and was baptized (Verse 31.) Then the churched throughout all Judea, Galilee and Samaria had peace and were edified. And walking in the fear of the Lord and in the comfort of the Holy Spirit, they were multiplied.

Appoints Officers

The Holy Spirit in the church appoints officers. "From Mellitus He sent to Ephesus and called for the elders of the church…Therefore take heed to yourselves and to all the flock, among which he the Holy Spirit has made you overseers, to shepherd the church of God which He purchased with His own blood" (Acts 20:17, 28).

"And when He had called His twelve disciples to Him, He gave them power over unclean spirits, to cast them out, and to heal all kinds of sickness and all kinds of disease… do not go into the way of the Gentiles and do no enter a city of the Samaritans. But go rather to the lost sheep of the house of Israel. And as you go, preach, saying the kingdom of heaven is at hand. Heal the sick, cleanse the lepers, raise the dead, and cast out demons, freely you have received, freely give" Mathew 10: 1,5-8

Paul and Barnabas were sent as missionaries in Acts by the Holy Spirit.

"Now separate to me Barnabas and Saul for the work to which I have called them… so being sent out by the Holy Spirit, they went down to Seleucia and from there they sailed to Cyprus" (Acts 13:2).

In the Old Testament, when God saw the disobedience of the people of Nineveh, he sent Jonah the son of Amittai to warn them. Though Jonah tried to escape to Tarshish, he later found himself in the belly of the Shark and repented. He obeyed God and the entire city was saved. (Read the book of Jonah).

Jesus Christ put Peter in charge of the Jews (see John 21:13, 17). And Paul was commissioned and sent to the Gentiles (Acts 13:46-49).

Direct Missionaries:

Missionaries are often exposed to assault and persecution in the cause of carrying out their work. Consider Paul's experience in Acts 13:10 12 with Bar Jesus, friend of Sergius Paulus, a proconsul who sought to hear the word of God. Unfortunately, Elymas the sorcerer withstood him, seeking to turn the proconsul away from the faith, but because Paul the Missionary was filled with the Holy Spirit he discerned his intentions and rebuked him by calling him an enemy of righteousness. Missionaries are sent by God's special direction, because of the dangers associated with the task. God's special direction, because of the danger associated with the task. God personally sent me from Tripoli, Libya North Africa, in the month of December 2004, to come to Nigeria shortly for a missionary work in Emaudo, Ekpoma and entire Nigeria. And I was instructed to serve with Divine Light Ambassadors Church (DLAC) (Favor Chapel) Nigeria under the leadership of Apostle Bernard Edehomon. This lasted for period of 15 years. Thereafter to take the Gospel of Christ to other parts of the world as stated in the book of Isaiah.

I will set a sign among them and those among them who escape. I will send to the nations.

To Tarshish and Pul and Lud, who draw the bow, and Tubal and Javan to the coastlands afar, who have not heard my fame nor seen my glory. And they shall declare my glory among the Gentiles" (Isaiah 66:19-21).

The above scriptures verse is where the Lord divinely led me to after he had called and commissioned me into the ministry in 2001. When I came to Nigeria in 2004 December I had problem with the weather, but the Lord delivered me and I went to Abuja to meet my friends at Abuja. When I was praying, the Holy Spirit directed me to go to Ekpoma and start my ministry from my house, witnessing for Christ. By His special grace, many people in my home town got converted and were baptized by total immersion, and are now members of local churches.

Phillip was directed by the Holy Spirit to the Ethiopian Eunuch in Acts "Then the Spirit said to Phillip, go near and overtake this chariot" (Acts 8:29).

The Holy Spirit is the one that leads while we follow, without Him, we are not working for God but ourselves and it leads to disappointments and pains. See how Phillip shared scriptures with the Eunuch and enabled him to receive the Lord Himself into his heart and he requested be baptized, after he believed the good news of our Lord Jesus Christ.

Since I was called into the ministry and commissioned, the Holy Spirit has always directed me to streets, places to minister, to the sick and the perishing souls/backsliding souls and our God who is the Lord of harvest has never failed me one day. All we need is obedience. One morning while I was in Emaudo, after my morning devotion, I was just entering my room to kneel and pray, but the Lord turned me back to go to Uwen-Emaudo and witness to people about Him. Behold the first person I met was a person contemplating suicide. I preached the gospel to him, counseled him and prayed for him. He confessed his sins and was free. The Holy Spirit comforts the church.

"Then the churches throughout all Judea, Galilee, and Samaria had peace and were edified. And walking in the fear of the Lord and in the Comfort of the Holy Spirit they were multiplied" *(Acts 6:7, Acts 11:21, 24).*

"The word of God spread, and the number of disciples multiplied greatly in Jerusalem, and a great many of the priests were obedient to the faith" (Acts 6:7).

The ministry of the Holy Spirit in the church is of great importance in all ramifications

SANCTIFIES THE CHURCH

The Holy Spirit has a great deal of ministry. He also sanctified the church "That I might be a minister of Jesus Christ to the Gentiles ministering the gospel of God, that the offering of the Gentiles might be acceptable, sanctified by the Holy Spirit". (Romans 15:16).

Christians are sanctified by the word of God through our Lord Jesus Christ by the power of the Holy Spirit.

"Sanctify them by your truth. Your word is truth" (John 17:17). Apostle Paul, formally called Saul was sanctified through the power of the Holy Spirit on his way to Damascus, in order to persecute the Christians. And he received the Lord instantly as he fell under the anointing speechless and was commissioned for the mission to go and deliver the Gentiles from darkness to light, and from the power of Satan to God, that they may receive forgiveness of sins and inheritance among those who are sanctified in me" (Acts 26:17, 18).

Apostle Paul uses this word in his salutation speech to the Corinthians' church.

"To the church of God in Corinth, to those sanctified in Christ Jesus and called to be holy, together with all those everywhere who call on the name of our Lord Jesus Christ their Lord and ours" I Corinthians 1:2 (NIV).

Because the Holy Spirit always sanctifies His church, we often use it in our benediction prayer: A biblical example is 1 Thessalonians 5:23

"May God himself, the God of peace sanctify you through and through, may your whole

Spirit, soul and body be kept blameless at the coming of our Lord Jesus Christ (NIV).

When the Holy Spirit sanctifies us, we receive divine ability to obey His commands and abstain from all appearances of evil, also from all forms of presumptuous acts the lead to defilement. Through the Holy Spirit, the God of peace sanctifies us or sets us apart wholly for His service and will (Also see John 17:7)

CHAPTER SIX
THE WORK OF THE HOLY SPIRIT IN SALVATION

The Holy Spirit brings to us convictions about Christ and acceptance of His work of salvation, not by the eloquent speech of a messenger!

Nor by works of righteousness which we have done, but according to His mercy He saved us, through the washing of regeneration and renewing of the Holy Spirit *, whom He poured out on us abundantly through Jesus Christ our savior"* (Titus 3:5-6).

The Holy Scriptures says in verse 3-4 that we were sometimes foolish, disobedient, deceived serving diverse lusts and pleasures, living in malice and envy, hateful and hating one another. But after that, the kindness and love of God towards mankind came to us through our Lord Jesus Christ by the power of Holy Spirit. He justified us by His grace, we are made heirs according to the hope of eternal life.

We were once foolish as sinners (verse 3):

"O foolish Galatians! Who has bewitched you that you should not obey the truth, before whose eyes Jesus Christ was clearly portrayed among you as crucified" Galatians 3:13

All Christians are repented sinners, because we have all sinned. Through the preaching of Christ we became saved (See Hebrews 9:26-28), not by works, but salvation is received by faith (Acts 4:12; Genesis 15:6 Romans 10:9 Galatians 2:16). We were unwise, foolish, disobedient, and deceived (Titus 3:3:2 Corinthians 4:4): serving diverse lust and worldly pleasures (Galatians 5:19-21; Ephesians 2:1, 3). We all were once living in malice and envy, hateful and hating one another, but the manifestation of the Kindness and love of God toward mankind brought us out of our depraved conditions.

As a matter of fact, salvation is not by the works of righteousness which man does. It is not by merit (Titus 3:5, Ephesians 2:8-9). It is by God's mercy He saved us, by the washing of regeneration in the precious blood of Christ and the word (Colossians 1:14, 1 Peter 1:18,21) and renewing of the Holy Spirit.

"Most assuredly, I say to you, unless one is born of water and spirit he cannot enter the Kingdom of God (John 3:5).

Jesus said to Nicodemus, you must be born again, changing our mind and getting renewed in the spirit is the work of the Holy Spirit.

*"And do not be conformed to this world, but be transformed the renewing of your mind, that you may prove what is that good and acceptable and perfect will of God". (*Romans 12:2)

Any man/woman that has accepted Jesus as Lord and person savior, needs to put on the new man which was created according to God, in true righteousness and holiness (Ephesians 4:24). This is what the Holy Spirit showers on us abundantly day by day through Jesus Christ. He grace justifies us; makes us heirs of the hope of eternal life.

"Being justified fully by His grace through the redemption is in Christ Jesus" (Roman 3:24)

(Also see Romans 51, 11; and Ephesians 2:8-9).

We can see how Apostle Paul's Life was transformed through power of the Holy Spirit that was at work in him, his entire life changing for good.

Personally, I was once a fornicator, smoker, drunkard and involved in cultism, and raised in idolatrous home, but as I became hungry for His word, the Holy Spirit came into my life and changed me and I became a different man. I used to be known for evil, but when I serve our Lord in the newness of the Spirit. The Bible says old that things are passed away.

"Therefore, if anyone is in Christ, he is a new creation; old things have passed away; behold, all things have become new" 2 Corinthian 5:17.

CHAPTER SEVEN
THE WORK OF THE HOLY SPIRIT IN THE SCIPTURE

Through the power of the Holy Spirit, the prophets speak God's mind and prophesying and interpreting prophecy. In Acts 28:25, Paul in his last message to the Jews turned to the Gentiles and testified that the Holy Spirit had inspired Isaiah the prophet (2 Peter 1:21; Acts 3:21; Heb. 1:1)

God's word is pronounced; the responsibility is with the people who heard the word, not many people act on it by faith. All heard the things that Paul declared, but not all believed. The responsibility is with us, not God or His word. God has created us a free moral agent, you can decide to believe the gospel or not. God is never responsible for the faith of some and the unbelief of others.

Our human heart is the problem, it is always deceiving us, since we permitted it to wax gross (blind) to the truth and closed against sound doctrine.

"And you shall know the truth, and the truth shall make you free" (John 8:32)

God doesn't force any man to do His will nor turn away any from doing His will, but Satan is responsible for all disobedience (2 Corinthians 4:4). The human and satanic action is rebellion against God and His word. Man has been given the free will to reject. Satan and turn to doing the will of God by humbling themselves before God, so they may get healed and be converted.

"That if you confess with your mouth the Lord Jesus and believe in your heart that God has raised Him from the dead, you will be saved. For with the heart one believes unto righteousness and with the month confession is made unto salvation..." (Romans 10,9,10)

The work of the Holy Spirit in the scriptures is powerful and prophecies from the scriptures concerning the gentiles have been fulfilled. The gentiles have been made equal with the Jews through faith on the scriptures.

"Then Paul and Barnabas grew bold and said "It was necessary that the Word of God should be spoken to you first: since you rejected it and judged yourself unworthy of everything life behold, we turn to the Gentiles."

Apostle Paul revealed that the Jews refused the Gospel.

"But when they opposed him and blasphemed, he shook his garment and said to them, "your blood be upon your own head; I am clean from now on, I will go to the Gentiles"...(Acts. 18:16).

Through the help of the Holy Spirit, the apostles were able to choose Mathias as a replacement of Judas Iscariot, as prophesied in the book of psalms (Psalms 109:8) Acts 1:15,20: Before this, Judas was a Bishop (Gr. Episkope)

Act 1:20. Unfortunately his sin made him to loose his office. The number of men that the Jews require to form a council as regards verse 20 was one hundred and twenty (see verse 15). It is very clear in the scriptures that Judas has actually obtained part in the Ministry, but by transgression he fell. (Acts 17:17,20, and 25).

"Jesus answered them. "Did I not choose you, the twelve and one of you is a devil?" (John 6:70).

To learn more about Judas see Psalm 109:1-20. Judas fell mutilating himself Acts: 1:19,19 and the Pharisees used his money to purchase a piece of land where he was buried (Mathew 27:5,8) having his habitation desolate and his name blotted out of the book of life.

The Holy Spirit is a powerful person behind the scripture hence: "All scripture is given by inspiration of God and is profitable for doctrine, for reproof, for correction for instruction in righteousness" 2 Timothy 3:16 (AKJVT) by Finis Lennings Dake.

With the power of the Holy Spirit the Holy Scriptures is given by inspiration (Greek Theopneusto) means: God's breath. This was a special influence of the Holy Spirit on the lives of holy men. He enabled them to continue the word of truth, so it could be profitable to all through teaching and reproof. Evidences are a means of rescue to all in their proper use and place in correcting false theories and practices like heresies etc.

Through the power of the Holy Spirit the scriptures are used in teaching mankind true righteousness and perfecting the man of God and imparting him with spiritual gifts for all good works (2 Timothy 3:16-17;2,9,21).

The Holy Spirit makes His word in our lives to destroy every attack of the enemy.

"And take the Helmet of salvation and the sword of the Spirit which is the word of God". (Ephesians 6:17).

The sword of the Spirit is the living word of God. it is a part of believer's armour. Sword is offensive armour for conquest, it enables you to destroy the enemy and bring him to surrender. Besides the sword are other weapons of offense as follows: spear, lance, battle axe, club, bow and arrows etc.

CHAPTER EIGHT
HOW TO RECEIVE THE HOLY SPIRIT

We learnt about the Holy Spirit baptism of Jesus Christ, and how the early disciples believed the word of the Lord and acted on it by faith, and the Holy Spirit at Pentecost came upon one hundred and twenty people who were praying and were all baptized with divine power.

"And they were all filled with the Holy Spirit *and began to speak with other tongues, as the spirit gave them utterance"* (Acts 2:4).

The Holy Spirit has come to stay permanently right from the day of Pentecost till date. All believers are to receive Him by faith and begin to exhibit the power of the Almighty God. Thus, the Holy Spirit is the means that God uses to call us into His grace (Galatians 1:15, 1 Thessalonians 1:5).

We receive the message of the gospel through the conviction power of the Holy Spirit (2 Thessalonians 2:14). The Holy Spirit moves through the word of God that we preach to save lives. How then shall they can on Him of whom they have not heard? And how can they hear without a preacher?

Cornelius, a Roman centurion who feared God (Acts 10:1,2) was a typical example, he received a vision from God to send for Peter who would teach him God's word and lead him and his household to Christ.

Peter, the servant of God preached the good news to Cornelius and his household in the power of the Holy Ghost (Acts 10:23, 43). While Peter was still preaching his sermon, the Holy Spirit took pre-eminence and fell on them all instantly, they receive the Holy Spirit by faith and spoke with tongues (Acts 10:44, 46).

Similarly, at Pentecost, when the one hundred and twenty people with the twelve Apostles were together in one accord, waiting by faith for the promised Holy Spirit, they receive a great visitation and began to speak in other tongues. The Holy Spirit came upon them liberally because they acted in faith. Thus after Cornelius had received the baptism of the Holy Spirit, those of the circumcision (Jews), who believed were astonished, because many of the Gentiles with Peter had receive the gift of the Holy Spirit and they heard them speak with tongues, magnifying God (Acts 10:45,46). Peter commanded them to be baptized in water (verses 47,48), Also, in Ephesus, Paul met some twelve disciples of Christ who had not received the power of the Holy Spirit and Discovered that God's divine power was missing in them. So, Paul laid his hands upon them and they received the power of the Holy Spirit and began to speak with other tongues and also prophesied (Acts 19:6-7).

To receive the Holy Spirit is very simple-act in faith like Cornelius and the people of

Ephesus. They opened their heart clearly for the word of God and the Holy Spirit rested upon them.

STEPS TO RECEIVING THE HOLY SPIRIT:

You must be born again:- The basic condition to receiving the indwelling of the Holy Spirit is true and genuine repentance.

"The spirit of truth, whom the world cannot receive, because it neither sees Him nor knows Him; but you know Him, for He dwells with you and will be in you. I will not leave you orphans; I will come to you" (John 14:17,18).

The worldly people do not have the privileged to the Holy Spirit, except they are renewed – first born again in Christ Jesus. This was what made Peter in his sermon on Pentecost to exhort them to be born again.

Total Submission:

When one continued to live with some un-confessed sins or evil covenants as regards family line- this can serve as hindrance to receiving the Holy Spirit. He is holy and does not dwell in hostility or filthy environment. People of this category, who still visit witch doctors, keeping idols, having evil covenant like soul tie relationship, dedication of their baby to river gods/goddess during conception, drugs addiction and belonging to cult while still in church, all need to be delivered.

All those rubbish are hindrance and blockage to the Holy Spirit in accessing our lives. Simon was formerly a sorcerer for a long time, but when be believed, after Phillip preached the gospel of the Kingdom of God, he believed. Both men and women were baptized, including Simon. After this baptism of water, Peter and John were sent to Samaria to necessitate the Holy Spirit impartation through the word. Then they laid hands on them, and they received the Holy Spirit (Acts 8:17). When Simon saw this, that through laying on of the Apostles hands the Holy Spirit was given, he offered them money, saying, *"Give me this power also, that anyone on whom I lay hands may receive the* Holy Spirit *(Verse 19).*

Peter rebuked him openly, having seen that his heart was full of all deceit and wickedness. There are some people like Simon today in our churches who need serious deliverance, the miracle seekers or Church prostitutes, running from one church to another, looking for miracles, when they have not surrendered their lives to Christ as Lord and personal savior of their lives! These people still hold on to demonic clutches on their hands, which stand as hindrance for the Holy Spirit baptism in their life.

As Apostle Paul preached in Ephesus, many believed and turned to Jesus Christ. Among those that believed were many who practiced magical arts. For this set of people in the church today to receive the baptism of the Holy Spirit and be successful spiritually financially and physically, they need to renounce their past involvement with idols and totally commit their life to our Lord Jesus Christ only. We cannot serve God and mammon!

As soon as they confessed their sins and turned from it, they got filled with the Holy Ghost and became useful vessels in God's hand and the word of God grew in the land (Acts 19:19-20).

FAITH IS NECESSARY

Faith is the major requirement for our Christian walk with our Lord Jesus Christ. After you have accepted the Lord Jesus as your lord and personal savior and are born again, by faith, you must count it Joy that you have been free from every evil oppression- fear, anxieties, bad dreams, spiritual sexual intercourse, poverty sickness, rejection etc. all you need to do is to ask in faith for the power of the Holy Spirit because He is already available for all to receive, but you must ask in faith. *So I say to you, ask and it will be given to you... for every one who asks receives... how much more will your heavenly father give the* Holy Spirit *to those who ask Him". (Luke 11:9-13).*

We do not need to be afraid to ask from our Lord Jesus, He is a cheerful father who loves us and has died for our sins. As a child of God, born of His Spirit and in His image/likeness we do not need to shy away from asking anything because God has not given us the spirit of fear but of power, love and sound mind (2 Timothy 1:7)All we need is just to be positive and specific in our request as children of God. As we do this, we shall have a positive result to our request and petition. And the Holy Spirit will come into your life and you shall commence speaking in diverse tongue.

I am a good example, when I gave my life to Christ I did not speak in tongues immediately, because the faith to speak in tongues was not yet activated in me until I took a bold step of faith. Immediately after I had my water baptism by total immersion by Apostle Bernard Edehomon, Head of Mission DLA Church (Favor Chapel) Nigeria, I spoke in diverse tongues the next Sunday service slowly, then I confided in my Senior Pastor about my feelings, and he encouraged me to have faith and speak it aloud and as I did it, I discovered myself in a spiritual realm of speaking without stopping. Praise the Lord!

Actually before this immersion baptism, I had formally received a wrong baptism by sprinkling and confirmation at the Roman Catholic, Mary the Queen Catholic Church, Ekpoma. By faith after much study on baptism, coupled with my friend's advice, Jayamma, a born again believer, who now is my wife, I receive total freedom. I got filled with the Holy Spirit with the evidence of speaking in tongues, Hallelujah! The Holy Scripture reveals that immersion baptism is the real baptism; see Colossians 2:12 and Romans 6:3-14. It is the type of baptism that Jesus had, in Mathew 3:13-17. *When He had been baptized. Jesus came up immediately from the water; and behold, the heavens were opened to Him, and He saw the Spirit of God descending like a dove and alighting upon Him"* (Mathew 3:16).

Faith is all we need to become what God destines us to be in life, faith brings an amazing fast result. Without faith, no man can please God, for He is the rewarded of those that diligently seek Him (Hebrew 11:6) "Now faith is the substance of things hoped for, the evidence of things not seen" *(Hebrew 11:1) KJSB by C.I. Scofield. Page. 1301.*

Remember that a doubtful person can never receive from our Lord Jesus Christ - like Peter doubted in his heart and sank in the sea. The moment faith came and he cried out to Jesus, he was lifted up. John the Baptist doubted Jesus Christ when he was in the prison and he was beheaded and served on a platter. It is dangerous to doubt God's person and ability. See James 1:17 God is the giver of gifts and His gifts are pure, perfect and good. *"Every good gift and every perfect gift is from above and comes down from the father of lights, with whom there is no variation or shadows of turning".*

And no one can say Jesus is Lord except by the Holy Spirit (1Corinthians 12:3b)

We need to welcome the Holy Spirit into our lives, homes and businesses, to have a fellowship and take a permanent residence in our lives. And as the divine power of the Holy Spirit comes upon us, we must allow Him to take absolute control over all our body and entire being. When the Holy Spirit comes upon one's body your body will become God's dwelling temple- and you shall be decorated with divine power, you can speak in tongues expressly without reservation on babbling of words. You will see yourself refreshed with the holy aroma.

Remember that speaking in tongues is very essential in ministry, because it edifies the body of Christ, the household of faith. See Jude 20, 1 Corinthians 14:14. Kathrine Kulmah, an amazing woman of God, received the anointing and power of the Holy Spirit and was distinguished alongside other top Christian leaders in the world today due to her love for the displaced ones in the society, she yielded herself to the Holy Spirit and was used mightily to heal many in the world. We are advised in 1 Corinthians 14:1 to pursue love, and desire spiritual gifts, but especially that you may prophesy.

Speaking in tongues is the evidence of the Holy Spirit indwelling a believer's life; it also shows the sign of a living church of Christ. This is because the early disciples after the Holy Spirit baptized them, they spoke in other tongues. This promise was proclaimed by our Lord in Mark 16:17.

"And these sign will follow those who believe! In my name they will cast out demons". If you read verse 16 you will learn that without believing by faith in Jesus, this cannot take place. Probably a lot of Christians who are baptized in water yet have not received the Spirit have no faith to receive. Such persons will never have the baptism of the Holy Spirit until they have faith to receive.

Faith is very vital, the early apostles or disciples by faith spoke in tongues after the baptism of the Holy Spirit, believing in the word of God (Acts 2:4, 10:46).

When the Holy Spirit gives you utterance, then you must speak it by faith-because the Holy Spirit cannot help you to speak it out. You need to activate it by faith and you will see yourself speaking in tongues. You need to continue to pray in the Spirit. *"Praying always with all prayers and supplication in the Spirit, being watchful to this end will all perseverance and supplication for all the saint"* Ephesians 6:18.

Praying in the Holy Spirit is very important. It is part of your fight against spiritual powers of evil. A continued, strong and incessant pleading with tongues brings a quick answer to your prayer

(Luke 18:1-8). Without this kind of prayer, the Christian armour will be ineffective (Mark. 13:33; Luke 21:36; Hebrew 13:17). The best way to pray is, praying in tongues. When you pray in tongue you will be edified spiritually.

"He that speaketh in an unknown tongue edified himself" (1 Corinthians 14:4, TKJSB. By C.I. Scofield) page 1224.

Speaking in tongue is also the best way you can worship God in the name of our Lord Jesus Christ.

"For he that speaketh in an unknown tongue speak not unto men, but unto God, for no man understandeth him; howbeit; in the Spirit he speaketh mysteries" 1 Corinthians 14:2, TKJSB By C.I. Scofield).

As you begin to pray in an unknown tongue, the Holy Spirit comes to unleash his power over the devil, which is always contending with you. And immediately you will be released and refreshed. Believers can speak in an unknown tongue and also sing in an unknown tongue (1 Corinthians 14:15). The moment you are filled with the Holy Spirit and begin to speak in an unknown tongue, you will regularly receive a message from the Lord.

Do not despite this gift of speaking in tongues, as many others do. The devil does not understand this language; it is a heavenly language.

The psalmist said in Psalm 81:10, "...open your month wide, and I will fit it:. The Holy scripture has also declared in Mathew 7:7: "If you then, being evil, know how to give good gifts to your children, how much more will your heavenly father give the Holy Spirit to those who ask Him".

CHAPTER NINE
RECEPTION OF THE HOLY SPIRIT

(a)   Promised: The Holy Spirit is the promise of God that came through our LORD Jesus Christ and has been freely given to all believers around the world, those who have put their trust in God.

This promise was given in prophesy to believers in the book of Joel. *"And it shall come to pass afterward, that I will pour out my spirit men shall dream dreams your young men shall see visions. And also upon the servants and upon the handmaids in those days will I pour out my Spirit"*. (Joel 2:28-32).

The scriptures talk about the spiritual restoration of all people (Israel) as in verse 18 during which period all the enemies that stand against God's people shall be destroyed through the help of the Holy Spirit's outpouring.

Peter said to them, Repent, and let every one of you baptized in the name of Jesus Christ for the remission of sins; and you shall receive the gift of the Holy Spirit for the promise is to you and your children and all who are afar off, as many as the Lord our God will call" Acts 2:38-39.

Anyone who believes receives because; it's a promise to generations of the earth. (See Mark 16:16).

(b). After Christ was glorified: Prophet Joel prophesied in Joel 2:28-32 about the promise Holy Spirit, but that prophesy was no fulfilled until

Christ died and was raised from the dead and glorified then the Holy Spirit was given.

"He who believes in me, as the scripture has said, out of his heart will flow rivers of living water. But this He spoke concerning the spirit, whom those believing in Him would receive for the Holy Spirit was not given, because Jesus was not yet glorified". (John 7: 38, 39).

Any man, in every race and generation can benefit from this prophecy and experience the "rivers of living waters" At Pentecost the Holy Spirit came down on the whole people that were present, and they began to speak with other tongues as the Spirit gave them utterance.

The Holy Bible said in Acts 2:7 that the onlookers were all amazed and marveled, saying to one another, *"look, are not all these who speak Galileans?* All tribe and nation of the earth were present and they heard then speaking with other tongues. The apostles whom the lord had filled with the Holy Ghost and power preached a powerful sermon that pricked the heart of the Jews.

"Therefore let all the house of Israel know assuredly that God has made this Jesus, whom you crucified, both Lord and Christ". (Acts 2:36).

He demonstrated the power of God through the Holy Spirit. This was the same Peter who denied Jesus Christ three times and went back to fishing, but because then the Holy Spirit had not come, he behaved cowardly. Now you can see a great difference between a man with the Holy Spirit and another without the Holy Spirit. Peter preached with great power and anointing of the Holy Spirit until people began to ask: *What shall we do?* "He said to them: *"Repent and let every one of you be baptized in the name of Jesus Christ for the remission of sins;, and you shall receive the gift of the Holy Spirit for the promise is to you and to your children, and all who are afar off. As many as the Lord our God will call"* Acts 2: 38.39.

Those who believed and were devoted to the faith received the Holy Ghost and they became witnessed for our LORD Jesus Christ with boldness and power of the Holy Spirit. Shame and fear departed from them.

The Gospel is not just about words; it is about activities of the Holy Spirit with the demonstration of power. Acts 2:46-47. The primary responsibility of the Christian life is prayer, witnessing and church fellowship (1 Thessalonians 5:17: 1 Thessalonians 1:5).

Special miracles happened through Peter in Acts 15-16. Even his shadow healed the sick and cast out demons.

After the disciples had prayed, the place where they were assembled together was shaken, and they were all filled with the Holy Spirit and they spoke the word of God with boldness (Acts 4:31).

In Acts 3:19-21, Peter witnessed with great power to the Jews during his days. That was the period of restoration spoken of by the prophets. This is also applicable to us today. With the authority of the name of Jesus, given to every Christian, our ministries can be an extension of the ministry of Christ.

Conditions for receiving the Holy Spirit

1.   Believe on Jesus Christ: If any one believes in Christ and obeys the message of the whole gospel, that person shall receive the Holy Spirit (Mark 16:15-20; Luke 24:49: Acts 1:4-8) The Word "believeth" denotes the act and process of faith and is the present tense of "pistis" We need to continue in faith in order to get the benefits of the Holy Spirit (Acts 14:22; Heb 10:23-38). Out of the believer will flow unlimited power to do the works of Christ!

2.   **Thirst:**   (John 7:37, Psalm 42:2; 63:1; 143:6; Isaiah 44:3). This means having a strong desire for complete union with God and the fullness of the Spirit. Come and walk with Jesus Christ: surrender your life to Jesus Christ to do His whole will.

3.   **Faith** (John 3:15) Greek, "**Pisteuo**" placing total confidence and absolute dependence upon and reliance in the word of God and of Jesus Christ (Ephesians 3:12, Philippians 1:6; Mathew 8:8-10 Romans 10:17; Hebrews 11:1-6).

4.   **Drink** (John 7:37) This means the whole hearted reception of the gift of the Holy Spirit into one's life in order to bear fruit for God and manifest the presence of the Holy Spirit (1 Corinthians 12:4-13); Galatians 5:22-23; Revelation 22:17).

Received Gentiles

(Acts 10:45): The conversion of Cornelius and the Holy Spirit falling on those who heard the word was a sign to Jews that the Gentiles were no longer to be treated as those who are not worthy to hear or obey the Gospel (Acts 10:44).

The scripture disclosed in Acts 11:18- When they hears these things they became silent and they glorified God, saying, then God has also granted to the Gentiles repentance of life.

Through the grace of our LORD JESUS CHRIST the gentiles were saved in the same manner having the circumcision of the heart, not literally (Acts 15:11). The Jews were astonished because they never believe that God would ever give such gift as the Holy Spirit to the Gentiles, as He gave the Jews at Pentecost (Act 10:45; 11:15-17; 15:8-9).

Though the Jews contended with Peter in Acts 11:2, but the Bible reveals in Romans 3:30 that there is one God who will justify the circumcised by faith and uncircumcised through faith.(Note Romans4:9-12; 15:8; Galatians 27-12; Philippians 3:3; Colossians 4:11 Titus 1:10). This is the reason why the Jews were aware that the Gentiles has received the same Holy Spirit that they had received about eight years before at Pentecost (Acts 2:1-11; 10: 44-48; 19:1-7). This experience is a proof that the Holy Spirit may be given to men at the period of their conversion as in the case of the disciples at Pentecost (Acts 2:1-11); the Samaritans (Acts 8:12-23);and the Ephesians(Acts 19:1-7)This also proves that the Holy Spirit can be received before water baptism as in the case of Paul (Acts 9:17-18). Often you can receive the Holy Spirit after water baptism as in the case of our Lord Jesus Christ (Mathew 3:16-17).

Now you may question, saying should we baptize anyone who has already received the Spirit or not?. The answer is emphatically yes! (See Acts 9:17-18; Acts 10:44-48). Water baptism is for the remission of sins and the indwelling of the Holy Spirit can be experienced before water baptism. That not withstanding, those who received the Holy Spirit before water baptism are still on course and can experience God's work of forgiveness.

The fact remains that water baptism to new converts and the indwelling of the Holy Spirit is never forbidden, rather is a command that we must obey strictly, whether you have receive the Holy Spirit prior to conversion or not.

Peter commanded them to be baptized as new converts not to save the soul, but as an answer to a good conscience and an outward testimony of an inward grace (1 Peter 3:21; 1 John 5:6-8).

In other words it is a ceremony of identification with the death, burial and resurrection of our Lord Jesus Christ. We need to be planted, dipped, buried in water and be raised in His glorious body, free from sin and we need to receive the Holy Spirit by faith and newness of our spirit in order to live in a transformed life (Colossians 2:12).

The church must be very careful in the interpretation of the Gospel, knowing fully well the danger awaiting liars as disclosed in the dispensation of law and dispensation of grace.

Baptism is not done in the name of Jesus only, but our Lord Jesus Christ authorized us to baptize people who believe in Him in the name of the Father and of the son and of the Holy Ghost (Mathew 28:19). The three act together in unity. Christ authorized us to baptize believers in the name of the three members of the God-head (1 John 5:7) and not in His name only.

Do not grieve Him:
The Holy Spirit had prepared Cornelius in advance and sent for Peter in Joppa by sending an angel in Cornelius and gave him a vision (Acts 10:3-7, 22,30;11:19).

He dealt with Peter too, making him to go to the Gentiles and He gave Peter a vision (Acts 10:9-16; 11:5).

The Holy Spirit gave him specific instruction (Acts 10:19-20) The Holy Spirit can be sinned against (Mathew 12:31, 32). The Holy Spirit is a Divine Person that can be sinned against.

Every sin and blasphemy against the father and son can be forgiven but the sin against the Holy Ghost shall not be forgive men (Mathew 12:31), so we must be very careful lest we sin against Him either consciously or unconsciously. Believers and unbelievers alike could commit this sin.

Blasphemies: to speak evil of (Jude 8; Ephesians 4:31)

Reviling (1 Timothy 6:4; 2 Peter 2:11; Mathew 27:39)

Defamed: (1 Corinthians 4:13)

Insult by blasphemy (Mathew 12:31)

Blasphemed by the Presumption of men: Blasphemy is an insulting remark or curse, even attributing to Satan the work of the Holy Spirit. In today's contemporary Christianity where sin is prevalent among Christian groups or denominations, they speak against one another. Being judgmental is very dangerous. The Holy bible has warned us not to ascribe God's work to Satan. When an anointed servant of the Lord works miracles and casts out demons through the power of our Lord Jesus Christ, it is an amazing grace. Give God the glory. We often see other Christian groups becoming jealous, trying to ridicule the minister of God instead of them to give God glory and thank Him for His miraculous power of healing poured out for the liberation of the oppressed. We are expected to pray to God and ask Him to use him or her more. If you need God to use you in such manner you can pray to God and believe Him by faith instead of you to stay on the fence, condemning people that are used by God. Such act is bad because it is the work of the flesh (Galatians 5:19-21). Blaspheming other churches and believers is a sin. I see people castigating men of God like Prophet T.B. Joshua, Pastor Chris Oyakhilomen, Pastor David Oyedepo and the rest, I tell you, our Lord is the God of signs and wonders, He is ever faithful to His obedient and faithful servants and He will use them for greater works and exploit for His kingdom work on earth. If Jesus could be blasphemed and ridiculed because He cast out demons and they agitated that He did so by the power of Beelzebub (Mark 3:22-30; Luke 11:14-20) why do we need to worry about those who do not believe in the work of the Holy Ghost? Keep on following the work of the Holy Spirit, never you mind what people may say about them, for His testimony is greater than that of men.

If anybody heals in the name of Jesus Christ through the power of the Holy Spirit, it shows that God is the Almighty. Be careful my brothers and sisters as well as pastors and ministers in church politics in order not to belittle the work of the Holy Spirit. This is a very serious matter (see 1 Corinthians 12:4-11,28). The Spirit is grieved when we underestimate God's power or when we use our human senses to value the work of God, and give the glory due to His name to Satan; the Spirit is grieved at such situations.

When the disciples of Jesus Christ saw some people preaching they told Jesus Christ that someone was preaching and casting out demons in His mane, Jesus said "if they cast out demons in my name, it shows they are not against us, for he who is not with us is against us.

Christians must remember that the Spirit of God acts in unity, irrespective of denomination (see 1 Corinthians 12:11-31).

"For as the body is one and has many members, but all the members of that one body, being many, are one body, so also is Christ" (Verse 12).

Blasphemy is an unforgivable sin especially if it is done maliciously and knowingly in order to frustrate a minister or a believer (Hebrew 10:26-31, 1 Timothy 1: 13).

We must be patient, desiring to see the end in order to obtain the promise of God, our only

Judge. I am just like Abraham born into a family of idolatry/heathenism but separated for His work as it pleases God. When I returned back to Nigeria, December 2004, under the divine instruction of God through the power of the Holy Ghost to embark on the work of the "Great Commission" I first met with my brother in Lagos, the Senior Pastor of Divine Light Ambassadors Church (DLA Church) for spiritual talk and I left him for Abuja where God divinely instructed me in prayer to come to Ekpoma for witnessing from house to house, which I did obediently.

After the exercise, a lot of people turned to Christ, but few slanderers commented on my family background, saying my father and my twin brother were witch doctors, therefore, they would not accept Jesus Christ. A certain lady met them discussing it and immediately educated them on the need to accept Jesus Christ, since salvation is a personal thing, again, she made them understand that God does not hold us bound to our past sins, but He gives us a glorious future after our repentance. This alone stopped every doubt in their hearts and the Gospel prevailed in their lives. I don't know if you are one of those people who still commit this kind of sin of blasphemy. Repent and confess your sins and you shall be saved.

Insulted by the pride of men: The Holy Spirit presents the atoning work of Christ to the sinner. If the sinner now rejects and refuses to believe or accept, he is insulting the Holy Spirit, it means the whole work of Christ is a deception or lies and presents God with another plan of salvation (works).

The bible warns in Hebrew 10:29 saying: *"Oh how much worse punishment do you suppose, will he though worthy, who has trampled the son of God underfoot, counted the blood of the covenant by which he was sanctified a common thing, and insulted the Spirit of grace?*

If we regard Christ's death as a common thing, like the death of an ordinary person, it will be sin. And to deny the deity of Jesus Christ and the preciousness of His blood is to despise the witness of the Holy Spirit as declared in 1 John 5:8 **Disobedience of men:** when people rebel and annoy the Holy Spirit, it becomes a sin. Example from scripture is the backslidden Israelites, who were regarded by the Holy Scriptures as stiff-necked people. They left the only true God and turned to idol. The principles of God never change. The issue of people who are disobedient and rebellious against the Holy Spirit in our contemporary society is punishable with the right judgment as it was in the time of old.

The Holy Scripture revealed about Ananias and Saphira who rebelled against the Holy Spirit and were punished. We could be honest to this fact, and concluded that we are hindrances to ourselves through our constant disobedient and rebellion. Most often, when the Holy Spirit through God's Holy Scriptures gives us justify ourselves because of pride, so we refuse to make the necessary repentance that will establish us in faith. In a situation like this, we are expected to thankful to God for exposing our weaknesses.

Rebellion is as a result of vexation, murmuring and unnecessary complaining especially when we refuse to accept the place he gives us in the Body of Christ, rather, continuously we keep on complaining to the point of vexation. This is mostly common among leaders in churches. This could lead to murder or formation of faction against the pastor-in-charge and the entire body of Christ. It is very dangerous and God will strike such people who strive with His servants. *When they envied Moses in the camp, and Aaron the Saint of the LORD, the earth opened up and swallowed Dathan, and covered the faction of Abiram. A fire was kindled in their company; the flame burned up the wicked". (Psalm 106:16-17).*

Some people even like to hijack the ministry from the pastor in-charge but they always fail as a result of the shrewdness of their character.

Unbelief of men: Many people in their attitude of doubting God's word have resisted the Holy Spirit (Hebrew 3:19). The Holy Spirit quickens the conscience to do right but in our unbelief we deliberately resist His pleading and leading. *"You* *stiff-necked and uncircumcised in heart and ear! You always resist the* Holy Spirit *as your fathers did, so do you" (Acts 7:51).*

Also the Holy Spirit quickens us to speak to a soul to become a missionary to go to Bible College to live a separated life from sin, to give to the poor, but how often do we obey this leading of the Holy Spirit, instead we disobey by resisting his guidance.

Remember, the Holy Spirit has warned us in Genesis 6:3, saying: *My spirit shall not always strive with man"*

To resist the Holy Spirit for too long may make God turn us over to a reprobate mind. (Romans 1:24). Learn to have the full possession of the Spirit, let your heart stop resisting the Holy Spirit. Drop that unbelief that has rocked your life.
Insincerity of man: *"...How is that you have agreed together to test the spirit of the Lord:" (Acts 5:9).* Ananias and Saphira became victim of this (insincerity) in seeking to deceive their brethren; they were actually tempted and lied to the Holy Spirit. Of course this is very rampant today in the church of God; remember that God is slow to anger and everyone shall be judged on the last day. Grace has been given to you to repent; especially workers in the church of God, including pastors shall be the first to judged by God (James 3:1; 1Peter 4:17-19). Let us examine ourselves by reaffirming our faith in Christ Jesus.

We could be guilty of this type of sin if we pretend to our brethren that we are wholly devoted to God, but actually indulge in secret sins. We have to be very careful of professing to be holy before men that it is before the Lord. This could also be regarded as hypocrisy.

David said in psalm 51:10- *"Create in me a clear heart, O God..."*

Are you that brother or sister who stands in congregation before God's holy alter to say *"I surrender all"*, and yet go back to sin or in your heart, you are a hypocrite? Repent.

I want you to remember Gehazi who lied to his master, Elisha in 2 King 5:25-27 and became a leper as a severe punishment from God. There is greater danger in lying to the Holy Spirit.

Oswald J. Smith said: *"Every deception and exaggeration, every false impression intended to harm, and every lie to man is a lie to the Holy Ghost.*

Quenching the Holy Spirit: There is a solemn command from the Holy Scripture to all believers in 1 Thessalonians 5:19-23, which states: *Quench not the spirit"*

Just like one can put off a burning flame of fire, you can as well put off the burning flame of the Spirit (see Isaiah 4:4, and Mathew 12:20) He is called the *"Spirit of burning"*. To quench means to stifle or silence the operation of the Holy Spirit.

Anytime the Holy Spirit speaks to us through the word or conscience, we must obey, irrespective of the cost. When you constantly ignore the voice of the Holy Spirit, you will not longer be in agreement with Him and most probably it results in hardness of heart and leads to quenching of the spirit or separation. Those ministers who have refused to confess their weakness before the Holy Spirit easily fall out of faith, turning to heresies.

We have to be very careful to see that we do not fall victim of criticizing the manifestation of the Spirit when others come out to share their testimony or when the preacher begins to reveal your secret sins during service. This could be regarded as a sin that can quench the Spirit.

Grieved by the frivolity of men: Ephesians 4:30. The Holy Spirit always trusts us to resist and obey the Lord- failure to do so make Him very sad. When we refuse or fail to have confidence in Him, He is grieved.

"And grieve not the Holy Spirit of God, whereby are sealed". Ephesians 4:30.

For example, when a parent had trust in a child and later discovers that the child is stealing or joins himself with a secret cult, and he or she is rusticated from school, his or her parents will be grieved. The Holy Spirit is like a dove, very sensitive one easily frightened. In other words, the

Holy Spirit could also be grieved by an unprofitable conversation of believers.

"Let all bitterness and wrath, and anger and clamor and evil speaking be put away from you, with all malice" (Ephesians 4:31).

Verse 29. Let no corrupt word proceed out of your mouth, but what is good for necessary edification, that it may impart grace to the hearers.

Note: the spirit of God cannot join in the unprofitable talk, much less in evil speaking. So, watch the door of your lips.

Believers are to live in constant communion with the Holy Spirit free of sin in order not to grieve Him. People that are filled with the Holy Spirit are happy and solemn.

Contingent: Acts 2:38; 5:32 Peter told them: *Repent and be baptized every one of you, in the name of Jesus Christ, for the forgiveness of your sins, and you will receive the gift of the* Holy Spirit Acts 2:38 (NIV).

Whoever believes in our Lord Jesus Christ genuinely and has repented from his or her sins is baptized shall be saved. Baptism is the result of repentance. Baptism is a command for God's children- it is expected to be done in the name of the father, son and the Holy Spirit for the remission of our sins. We die with Christ and are clothed with Christ. Baptism is usually done by total immersion (Greek, Baptizo), to dip or plant. It symbolizes the believer's identification with the death, burial and resurrection of our Lord Jesus Christ (Mark 16:16; Mathew 28:19).

The gift of the Holy Spirit is given when a person meets the condition in Psalm 45:7,8 to love righteousness and hate iniquity. This gift of the Holy Spirit makes all to be one spirit. *"For by one spirit are we all baptized into one body, whether we be Jews or Gentiles,... and have been all made to drink into one Spirit". (1 Corinthians 12:13).*

This is the experience you shall have at conversion by the power of the Holy Spirit the new convert into the invisible body of Christ by the Spirit at conversion. Apostle Peter exhorted everyone to be *"filled with the Spirit"* not to grieve or quench the Spirit. The Pentecost experienced of the Holy Spirit (Acts 2:1-4) was the beginning of a new dispensation. According to J.O. Sanders:
Every believer has been baptize . "All baptized"
The experience is in the past tense. It is a completed transaction.
The function of this baptism is to place the believers "into one body"
It unifies believers, irrespective of the races, color or politics.

The book of Ephesians talks about one baptism (Ephesians 4:5). *"One Lord one faith, one baptism."* This is the same as in 1 Corinthians 12:13, *"for we are members of His body, of His flesh, and of His bones".*

Water baptism is the second type of baptism, which is commanded too as an earthly sign required by the church. God commands it. Baptism by fire can take place before water baptism or after water baptism as in the case of our LORD JESUS CHRIST in Matt. 3:16-17. Mrs. E.W. Wellers said that baptism of the Holy Spirit is an initial work that happens at salvation, meaning a complete identification with the savior.

She further explained, using Romans 6:3-11 as the only best definition of baptism of the spirit from the scripture. There is need to have faith in Christ at conversion in order to benefit from the gift of God. As a believer, you are:

Born of the spirit –John 3:3-8\

Received the true Spirit (Ephesians 1:14,2 Corinthians 1:22; 5:5)

Sealed with the Spirit (Ephesians 1:13; 4:30)

Indwelt by the Spirit (Romans 8:9)

Baptized into one body, a relational activity joining Christ and believers, irrespective of race and color/cultural difference (see 1 Corinthians 12:13).

Definition of Baptism according to Roman 6:3-11

Baptized into His death (Romans 6:3) "I am crucified with Christ" (see Galatians 2:20

Baptized into His burial (Rom 6:4) complete identification with His body.

Baptized into His resurrection (Roman 6:5), complete entry into His new body.

Baptized into His resurrected life (Roman 6:8), "live with Him," live in His body.

Through baptism we are complete in the new resurrected body of Christ (see Colossians 2:10-12).

Note that water baptism symbolizes also the church unity (1 Corinthians 12:13). Apostle Paul pointed this out when church unity was being threatened in Corinth by factions against one another when they started using the Christian freedom and spiritual gifts for selfish purposes by teachers to promote false doctrine (1 Corinthians1:11-13;3:1-4,8:11-12;11:18;14:3-4;16-17;15:12) Paul admonished then to put away rivalry and division, because himself and Apollos were co-workers and not rivals (1 Corinthians 3:5-9;4:1-7) he declared that the church is one body (1 Cor. 12:12-27); he pointed to the Lord's Supper (1Corinthains 11:23-29). He laid emphasis on the heart of the gospel which states: *"Christ died for our sins according to the scriptures, that he was buried, that he was raised on the third day"*... 1 Corinthians 15:3-4. The book of 1Corinthians put much priority on unity by using spiritual gifts for the benefit of all (1 Corinthians 12:7,14:4-5, 19).

CHAPTER TEN
GIFTS AND FRUIT OF THE HOLY SPIRIT

God gave gifts of the Holy Spirit; they are different from natural talents. This makes us to bear good fruits in our fields of ministry (1 Corinthian 12:8-10).

Kinds of Gifts:

The Gift of wisdom

Knowledge

Faith

Healing

Miracles

Prophesy

Discernment

Tongues

The gifts to interpret tongues.

According to 1 Corinthians 12:8 to one person is given the word of wisdom through the same spirit.

"For He himself gave some to be apostles, some prophets, some evangelists and some pastors and teachers for the equipping of the saints for the work of ministry for the edifying of the body of Christ, till we all come to the faith and of the knowledge of the Son of God, to a perfect man, to the measure of the stature of the fullness of Christ... from whom the whole body, joined and knit together by what every join supplies, according to the effective working by which every

part does its share, causes growth of the body for the edifying of itself in love" (Ephesians 4: 11-16).

Romans 12:6-8 adds of exhortation, gift if giving, gift of ruling and the gift of showing mercy. Increasing fruit bearing and possessing the character of Christ could easily identify abounding in every good work. The Holy Spirit as the director always takes the lead (see 1 John 2:27; 1 John 4:8).

FIVE FOLD MINISTRY: Ephesians 4:11-16
Apostles
Prophets
Evangelists
Pastors and
Teachers

These entire gifts are given by God to all men (1 Corinthians 12:11) and are to be used judiciously for the work of the ministry. It is the Holy Spirit that is responsible for placing new converts in the Body of Christ- endowing him or her for a particular location and field of ministry in the Body of Christ (Eph. 2:21, 22). No man has power to do this but God alone.

More also, gifts are given for the profiting of the body of Christ (1 Corinthians 12:7). *But the manifestation of the Spirit is given each one for the profit of all".*

At conversion, a soul is saved from the pit of hell. That is why we must all use our gifts individually to save and deliver many from bondage through the power supplied by the Holy Spirit of His sons. All parts of the body must carry out their functions. Spiritual gifts should be greatly desired by all.

"...But earnestly desire the best gifts". (1 Corinthians 12:31). We must never be satisfied with one gift, rather seek more of His fullness (God head) in order to become a complete vessel of God. Paul said that prophecy should be most desirable (1 Corinthians 14:1, 39). We must aspire for higher gifts, for certain position in the body of Christ. In Mathew 25:14-30 some were given one talent (gift), others two and others five and the one who received five gained more, while the one who received one talent buried his own in the ground. Note verse 28, the one whose gift multiplied to eleven gifts is the one that traded with his gift.

Everybody in Christ has spiritual gifts (1 Cor. 7:7,) your gifts must be used to the glory of God.

"Do not neglect the gift that is in you, which was given to you by prophecy with the laying on of the hands of the eldership" (1 Timothy 4:14).

We should not hide our gift like many others. They shy away from their gifts because they feel inferior before others. If we refuse to use the gift that is given to us by God, it will run away and then we will be in danger of judgment like the foolish steward in Mathew 25: 1 recommend for you "Covenant Blessing of Stewardship", a book by my senior pastor, Apostle Bernard Edehomon. For example, a soldier or police officer that was trained to shoot, if he leaves service for many years, he or she shall become inactive and lose the skill of shooting, which he or she formerly received from previous training.

We should also improve on our gifts by stirring the gift of God in us (2 Timothy 1:6). The gift of God needs a continuous practice for it to be more useful in God's kingdom. (also see Colossians 1:29).

KIND OF FRUITS

Love: Divine love is an attribute of GOD (1 John 4:16; 1 Corinthians 13).

Joy: Not the worldly type, but deep, gladness, Philippians 4:4

Peace: The peace of God that satisfies the soul completely, (Colossian 3:15).

Longsuffering (Patience): The natural men are impatient, saints (believers) are the opposite, and they should be patient in all they do.

Gentleness: (kindness or graciousness): Jesus was known by His graciousness.

Goodness (benevolence). This virtue makes the Christian full of good works.

Faith (faithfulness): He is dependable and can be relied on at all times.

Meekness (mildness of temper): He is humble, particularly true of us, 2 Timothy 2:25.

Temperance (Self control) moderate in drinking, appetite, dressing, habit and fashion.

God, as part of His plan for salvation divinely gives the gifts and fruits of the Holy Spirit to believers. By conversion, every believer possesses the Holy Spirit (see Rom 8:16) so, the Christian is incomplete until he/she manifests the nine fruits of the gracious Holy Spirit (Galatians 5:22-23).

Qualities

Fruits is an evidence of death…"*Unless a grain of wheat falls into the ground and dies, it remains alone: but it dies. It produced much grain". (John 12:24) if we are not dead we will merely bring forth the works of the flesh: spiritual fruits are the evidence of death to self. If you abide alone, it is a sign that you are not dead to self and will there fore not bear any fruit. The new life is capable of bringing forth fruit to the glory of God. Fruit is necessary for you to continue with God unto everlasting life.*

"Every branch in me that does not bear fruit. He takes away and every branch that bears fruit. He prunes, that it may bear more fruit". (John 15:2).

In Luke 13:9 the scripture says: *"And if it bears fruits, well. But if not, after that you can cut if down".*

The only reason for our existence here after conversion is, to bear fruit. The fruitless believer cannot enjoy the privileges of continuing with Christ because they will be cut off from the body of Christ. Fruitlessness and favor with God cannot stay together. Do away with barrenness and bear fruit for God. (see Luke 13:7, James 5:7,Galatians 5:22-23).

Fruit is what reveals the stuff you are made up of. *"The tree in known by its fruit"* (Mathew 12:33). The spies reported to Moses and Aaron and the whole Israelites community by presenting the fruit of the land to prove that the land was fertile (Numbers 13:26). The fruit portrayed by an individual proves the family he/she belongs, because sheep does not give birth to goat neither do grapes bear figs, thistles nor thorns (Mathew 7:16-20). The born again Christians are not expected to produce the work of the flesh (Gal 5:17-21). "Now *when vintage time drew near, he sent his servants to the vine dressers, that they might receive its fruit"* Mathew 27:34.

Fruits are not just for the tree but also for others to see and eat. Our good works must bless mankind and glorify God. We produce good fruit not for our own benefit but for God. He owns everything, all honors go to Him.

Every good fruit is from God *"Ephraim shall say, what have I to do anymore with idols? I have heard and observed him, I am like a green cypress tree; your fruit is found in me"- Hosea 14:8*

And except we abide in Him (Christ/) we cannot bear much fruit "*... For without me you can do nothing" John 15:5*

We must abide in Christ to be fruitful. *"Abide in Me, and I in you as the branch cannot bear fruit of itself. Unless it abides in the vine, neither can you, unless you abide in me". (John 15:4)*

The natural fruit is Adamic in nature (flesh) and it is wild and deadly. The born again Christian are rooted in Christ, so they have the glorious traits of Christ, this was Paul's prayer for the Ephesian Christians. *..."So that Christ may dwell in your hearts through faith. And I pray that you, being rooted and established in love, may have power, together with all the saints, to grasp how wide and long and high and deep is the love of Christ"* (Ephesians 3:17, 18).

If there is no spiritual fruit in our lives then there will be no reproduction of the virtue of Christ in others. The fruit helps us to witness about the Lord, we have been created by God to produce and bring forth fruit. (See Genesis 1:28).

Any Christian who cannot bear fruit is a hindrance to the Gospel. *"... Bearing fruit in every good work, growing in the knowledge of God." Colossians 1:10.*

Fleshy Fruit: *(Galatians 5:9-21)*

Adultery: Unlawful sexual relations between men and women who are married with another (single or married) (Mathew 5:32).

Fornication: **Same** as adultery above besides all manner of other unlawful relations (Mathew 5:32).

Uncleanness:- Whatever is opposite of purity, including sodomy, homosexuality, lesbianism, pederasty, bestiality and all other forms of sexual perversion (Galatians 5:19, Romans 1:21-32; 6:19; 2 Corinthians 12:21).

Lasciviousness: Licentiousness, lustfulness, unchastely and lewdness, lasciviousness (Mark 7:22; 2 Corinthians 12:21: Ephesians 4:19), wantonness (Romans 13:13 2 Peter 2:18). Lasciviousness is the promotion or parking of that which tends to produce lewd emotions, anything tending to foster sexual sin and lust. That is why many worldly pleasures have to be avoided by the Christians-so that lasciviousness may not be committed.

Idolatry: Image worship (1 Corinthians 10:4; Galatians 15:20; 1 Peter 4:3) Idolatry includes anything on which affections are passionately set; extravagant admiration of the heart (Ephesians 5:5; Colossians 3:5).

Witchcraft: Sorcery, practice of dealing with evil spirits; magical incantations and casting spells and

charms upon one by means of drugs and portions
of various kinds (Galatians 5:20; Revelation 9:21;
18:23).

CHAPTER ELEVEN
FILLED WITH THE HOLY SPIRIT

Our Lord Jesus Christ promised every Christian the Holy Spirit as a gift, we see a Pentecost the disciples filled with the Holy Spirit. The Holy Spirit is what qualified us as believers for service and for living a joy filled, victorious life and makes us more like Christ, *"And be not drunk with wine, where in is excess; but be filled with the Spirit (Ephesians 5:18)*

Apostle Paul commands Christians to be filled continually with the Spirit (1 Thessalonians 5:7) all the Christians (born again) have this privilege to receive the Spirit of Sonship and the Holy Spirit in measure (Roman 8:9, 14-16), but just a measure is not enough for you, if you will accept the truth and seek God for the fullness of the Spirit, you will experience an overflow of the Spirit. The unfilled Christian tongues have proofs of His presence.

The evidence of the indwelling of the Holy Spirit was in the life of our Lord Jesus and early Apostles as follows:

Jesus Christ (Luke 4:1)

Bezale (Exodus 31:2-3)

John the Baptism (Luke 1:15, 60)

Elizabeth (Luke 1:41)

Zechariahs (Luke 1:67)

Pentecost Christians (Acts 2:1-4)

Peter (Acts 4:8)

Seven men (Acts 6:3-5)
Stephen (Acts 7:55)
Barnabas (Acts 11:22, 24)
Paul (Acts 11:22, 24)
Certain disciples (Acts 13:52)

Every believer in Jesus Christ needs the indwelling of the Holy Spirit; this experience is for Apostles, preachers, fathers, mothers, young people and laborers. This is very important for our own benefit, as children of God (Christians), we need the Holy Spirit to be effective in our Christian service to God. This experience is an individual blessing: men are saved and filled individually. And it comes when we completely surrender our life to Him.

Three major areas the Holy Spirit is evident in believers today:

A joyful, melodious heart. "… Speaking to yourselves in psalms and hymns and spiritual songs, singing and making melody in your heart to the Lord" *Ephesians 5:19*. Example is Fanny Crosby, born on March 1823 in Southeast, NY USA, who lost her sight six weeks after her birth, through improper medication. Notwithstanding, fanny was filled with the Holy Spirit and never allowed anybody to pity her condition. She developed into extraordinary strength of character through the power of the Holy Spirit to write beautiful hymns and songs like: Blessed Assurance; Pass Me Not: Near the Cross: I am

Thine, O Lord; Close to Thee; To God be the Glory; Rescue the Perishing etc,

As for Fanny ridiculous comments from people never weighed her down even when a Scottish minister asked her. "I think it is a great pity that the master showered so many gifts on you but did not give you sight." She smiled at the question and answered, "Do you know that if at birth I had been able to make one petition to my creator, it would have been that I should be born blind? The minister asked why, she answered and said "Because when I get to heaven the first face that shall gladden my sight will be that of my Savior". And she died on February 11, 1915 to met the Lord our savior". Do you pity yourself because you are handicapped or do you excel in life in spite of your condition, fanny Crosby's spirit-filled life in Christ challenges us as Christians to live a joyful melodious life.

A thankful attitude:- *Giving thanks always for all things unto God and the father in the name of our Lord Jesus Christ" Ephesians 5:20.* In Ekpoma, at Winners Chapel, I saw a beautiful girl on wheel chair in the choir. She was thankful with smiles all over her face, worshipping God, not worried about her present state, but thankful always to God, she does not miss any church service. As a matter of fact, this is the type of life God want from every true believer and the Holy Spirit makes it possible.

A submissive spirit:- *Submitting yourselves one to another in the fear of God"* (Ephesians 5:21). The Book of Proverbs 14:26-27 put in this way: *In the fear of the LORD there is strong confidence and His children will have a place of refuge. The fear of the LORD is a fountain of life, to turn one away from the snares of death."*
Luke 1:50 says, *And His mercies are on those who fear Him from generation to generation.* When we are submissive to God's will and the leading of the Holy Spirit, it will manifest itself in submission to God and others. We must allow ourselves to be controlled by the guidance of the Holy Spirit.

In Marital homes for example " wives are to submit to their husband William Booth was filled with the Holy Spirit together with her husband William Booth (founder of the Salvation Army in 1865). She was born in England on January 17, 1829; Catherine loved the Bible and had read it eight times by the time she was twelve. She got born again at 16 and got married to William Booth at 26. They had eight children.

In marriage and ministry, she was a strong supporter of her husband; some of the other things she did to keep her marriage going for such a long time include her decision, because she allowed the Governor (Holy Spirit) to lead her life. She consciously recognized the Holy Spirit as being in full control of her life, completely governing every details of her life and ministry as follows:

She never hid any secret from her husband.

She never kept any secret savings which her husband did not know about.

She never quarreled or argued with her husband before their children. She died October 4, 1890.

So much of such godly characters is expected of you as a born again woman, young or old and married or single believer. You should be challenged by the life of Catherine Booth and her outstanding qualities through the prompting of the Holy Spirit, to read the Bible regularly. Re-affirm your faith to serve God in Spirit and in truth (John 4:24) and bring your marriage or relationship in good shape by being filled with the Holy Spirit, as you may adopt Catherine Booth's marriage style.

Equally, husbands are to love their wives-giving honor to their wives in self sacrifice as Christ gave Himself to the Church. Children also are to submit to and honor their parents in the Lord, honoring them is a command from God with a promise so that your days may be long (Ephesians 6:1-3) it is also the responsibility of the parents to bring up their children properly (verse 4). Slaves that are under authority are to be obedient to their own master (verses 5-8) as unto Christ. Masters are not to maltreat their servants unjustly too (verse 9).

We are called by Christ to live a life of Joy and thankfulness in submission to one another in the fear of the Lord, with the help of the Holy

Spirit this is very possible, just as the disciples were filled with Joy and the Holy Spirit (Acts 13:52). The church need have every member filled with the Holy Spirit; though many believers do silly (unwise) things today in the name of being filled with the Holy Spirit, yet we all need the Holy Spirit to be free from evil.

Tongues are very necessary in believer's lives and ministry it edifies the body and serves as a sign to the unbelievers. The spirit manifests the reality of the Gospel for the entire world to see 1 Corinthians 14:22.

The church needs spirit filled members absence of such people makes the church to continue in disorders, dissension, strife, backbiting, jealously and scandals, Galatians 5:19-21. It is very good for all members of the church to be Spirit filled, especially the pastor, elders, deacons, Sunday School teachers, ushers, securities, sanctuary keepers/vine dressers, choir members and new converts altogether.

The pastor and elders/deacons or deaconess need Him to offer a just administration in smooth running of the church. Remember the word of Jesus in Mathew 5:48 which states: *"Therefore you shall be perfect, just as your father in heaven is perfect"*.

Believers would be ineffective if not filled. The work of the Lord is not based on emotion, feelings or flesh; otherwise it will lead us to disappointment or failure. This is why many ministries are folding up. their intention of going into the ministry was never divine, rather it was based on carnality, so when temptation comes they are easily cut off, if God does not speak, they will run out of patience and go seeking the other way round as Saul did (see 1 Samuel 28:6-7).

The Spirit is never selfish nor looking for vain glory (his will) but God's will even when the church is facing temptation, the pastor should know that he is not doing his own work but the work of God and so he should pray to the Father and always remember Mathew 16:18 God is ever ready to build His church.

Believer's are to live the crucified life in Christ, and becomes effective in the Lord's hand to be able to reach out to sinners through the power of the Holy Spirit.

CHAPTER TWELVE
THE TWELVE BLESSINGS OF THE HOLY SPIRIT

Sets us free from sin: Romans 6:22 Greek work, *Iambano"* means, "to take in order to carry away". "to remove". *He Himself took our infirmities. And bore our sickness."* (Mathew 8:17). Also see Isaiah sickness upon one's self and carry it as His own"

Jesus Christ so loved us that He took our physical, mental or moral weakness or flaws away by the power of the Holy Spirit, that it might be fulfilled which was spoken by Isaiah the prophet, saying, *Himself took our infirmities and bore our sickness. Mathew 8:17.*

He redeemed us by removing our sins, also all sickness with complete redemption of the body as well as the soul. (Romans 8:11,7-24; Phil 13:21; Ephesians 5:27). Through the power of the Holy Spirit, Jesus Christ delivered us from sin and death as well as diseases (Isaiah 61:1, John 10:10) *"... with His stripes we are healed"* (Isaiah 53:5; Mathew 8:17; 1 Peter 2:24).

2. **Cancels Death Penalty:** *There is therefore now no condemnation to those who are in Christ Jesus , who do not walk according to the flesh but according to the spirit. For the law of the Spirit of life in Christ Jesus has made me free from the law of sin and death"* (Romans 8:1-2).

Prostitutes, armed robbers, adulterers, drugs addict all have their sins forgiven. They are free from death and plagues of death because the wages of sins is death. The moment they receive Jesus Christ into their heart they will be free from death penalty in Jesus name.

3. **Fulfils righteousness:** Mathew 3:13-15. The Holy Spirit came upon Christ Jesus in order to fulfill all righteousness and to be manifested to Israel. *"I did not know Him. But that He should be revealed to Israel, therefore I came baptizing with water… I saw the Spirit descending form heaven like a dove and He remained upon Him… I did not know Him, but He who sent me to baptize with water said to me, 'upon whom you see the Spirit descending and remaining on Him, this is He who baptized with the* Holy Spirit" (John 1:31)

Baptism is the only symbol of the **death, burial and resurrection** of Christ (1 Peter 3:21). Faith in the blood of Jesus Christ brings remissions of sins, (Mathew 26:28; Roman 3:24-28). Water baptism not essential to salvation (1 Corinthians1:13-21_) Old Testament saint including John and Luke 1:15,41,46,67,2:25-38 who were filled with the Spirit were saved without water baptism.

Christ forgave sins without baptism (Mathew 9:1-7, Luke 7:36-50; 18:9-14; 19:1-9; 23:43; John 4:49-53; 7:31; 8:30-31; 11:45; 12:11, 42: Acts 3:1-11, 16;4:10-12 etc).

John desired the Spirit baptism Christ came to give (John 1:31, 84). John was filled (Luke 1:15) but never baptized with the Spirit, the Spirit was not given until Christ was glorified (John 7:37-39; Acts 1:4-8; 2:23-34; 11:16).

Indwells believers (Romans 8:9-11) Jesus came that we may be renewed in the Spirit, body and mind 2 Corinthians 5:21; Ephesians 2:10;4:23,24, Proverbs 11:30; Galatians 5:22, Mathew 5:6.

TheHoly Spirit indwells believers so that they many no more set their mind on the things of the flesh, but of the Spirit. Anyone that does not have the Spirit is not of Christ, The Christians now have new Life and are dead to sin (2 Corinthians 5:17). The Holy Spirit quickens the mortal body (verse 11). Makes alive (1 Corinthians 15:22); gives life (2 Corinthians 3:6; Galatians 3:21) and quickens (John 5:21; 6:63 Roman 4:17; 8:11; 1 Corinthians 15:36, 45) flesh has no more control over our lives.

5.   Gives life (Rom 8:10) "And if Christ be in you, the body is dead because of sin; but the Spirit is life because of righteousness." If Christ is in you (2 Corinthians 5:17-18) the body is dead to all sin, and the Spirit dominates your life as you live to all righteousness.

Carnal Life	Spirit Life
Spirit dead to God	Spirit alive to God
No Christ	Christ in life (8:10)
Sinful life	righteous life

No Holy Spirit   Spirit indwelling
No body quickening   Quickening
Debtor to flesh   not debtor (8:12)
No help from spirit   help (8:13)
End is death Rom 8.6a End is life John 6:63;
Roman 6:8

6. Quickens the mortal body:- (Roman 8:11). *But if the spirit of Him that raised up Jesus from the dead dwell in you, he that raised up Christ from the dead shall also quicken your moral body by His spirit that dwelleth in you"* (The King James Reference Edition by C.I. Scofield, page, 1201.

Because the Spirit lives in you He quickens your moral bodied and makes alive all inactive cells of your entire being (1 Corinthians 15:22) the dead, at the coming of Christ shall be raised (made alive) given life (2 Corinthians 3:6; Galatians 3:21) and quickened (John 5:21; 6:23), so you are no longer under the control of the flesh. It has no control over you again. The spirit of Christ in you terminates all practices of the flesh. (see Romans 8:12-13), Galatians 5:16-26, Colossians 3:5-10)

Mortifies sinful members:- (Roman 8:13). *"For if ye live after the flesh, ye shall die; but if ye through the Spirit do mortify the deeds of the body, ye shall live"* (The King James Reference by C.I. Scofield, page 1201)

Carnal Life	Spirit Life
Of the mind, things of the flesh the spirit Rom 8:5	Things of
Carnally minded Spiritually dead Romans 8:6	Spiritually alive
Enmity with God God Romans 8:7	Friend of
Not subject to God God & His will	Subject to
Cannot be subject subject	can be
Cannot please God God Romans 8:8	can please
Not in the Spirit	In the spirit
Not Christ's Roman 8:9	Is Christ's
Body alive to sin	Body dead to sin

Leads children of God:- For as many as are lead by the Spirit, God they are sons of God". (Rom 8:14). We as children of God need to follow the leading of the Holy Spirit at all times. A good example from the scripture is Phillip. He followed the leading of the Spirit and converted the Ethiopian Eunuch *"...Go near and overtake this chariot"* (Acts 8:29).

9 . Adopt people into God's family:- *For ye have not received the Spirit of bondage again to fear; but ye have received the Spirit of adoption, whereby we cry. Abba father".* (Rom 8:15, Dake's Annotated reference Bible)

This is the first blessing, the outpoured Holy Spirit, upon all flesh. Romans 8:11, 16,23, 1 Corinthians 15:20,23:16:15; James 1:18; Revelations 14:4) as son, you no longer need to fear persecution victimization of family members who are unbelievers (see Romans 8:35, 37-39). You have the Spirit of Christ in you. That spirit rejoices over persecution, because in persecution we glory. You share the same rights and privileges as one born in the family, slaves were never allowed to call their master or mistress, father.

10.   **Bears witness of sonship:** *"The Spirit itself beareth witness with our spirit, that we are the children of God."* (Rom. 8:16).

As sons, we have the trait of Christ; born of the Spirit, loving like Jesus Christ, having social concern to reach out to the lost/perishing souls, witness Christ's love, repentance and forgiveness of sins.

11.   Helps infirmities:- *"Likewise, the spirit also **helpeth** our infirmities: for we know not what we should pray for as we ought; but the Spirit itself **maketh** intercession for us with **groaning** which cannot be uttered".* (Rom 8:26) *Dake's Annotated Reference Bible.*

We would make many mistakes in prayer if the spirit does not inspire us with prayer desires and help us fulfill those desires in the will of God. The Holy Spirit Himself is a personal and He is intelligent. He applies Himself to intercede for others. The Holy Spirit does this by the heart. *I have surely seen the oppression of my people who are in Egypt. I have heard their groaning and have come down to deliver them"* (Acts 7:34).

Also see Exodus 3:57,8,10. It is only Christ who knows the mind of the Spirit. He (Christ) is our intercessor when we pray, we join Him in intercession and He has sent the Holy Spirit down on all flesh to help us when we pray, because He knows the mind of the Spirit. All three persons of the Trinity search the hearts of men. God the father (1 Chronicles 28:9; Jeremiah 17:10), the son (Revelation 2:23) and the spirit (1corinthians 2:10).

12.   Makes intercession for the saints:- "Now He who searches the hearts knows what the mind of the Spirit, is because He makes intercession for the saints according to the will of God". (Romans 8:27).

The Holy Spirit intercedes; acts as an agent or manager in all aspect of salvation and dealings with God. "…who is even at the right hand of God, who also makes intercession for us" (Reference Hebrews 7:25 and Acts 25).

The Holy Spirit intercedes for Apostle Paul in charges to set him free when he was falsely accused.

God's providence is working on behalf of them who have God and who walk obediently according to His purpose. *"And they went out and preached everywhere, the Lord working with them and confirming the word through the accompanying signs. Amen! Mark 16:20.*

CHAPTER THIRTEEN
THE NAMES/ TITLES APPLIED TO THE HOLY SPIRIT

The names and titles attached to the Holy Spirit in the scriptures are so powerful and only few Christians knows these names and it is very important we apply these names and titles while because the three (Trinity) of them act in unity. So when we pray and refuse to apply all these names and titles in prayer, we simply pray using force in prayers, but it's the spirit codes that you need to call (the names/titles) to link you to heaven for urgent response. Here are some of the names/codes/titles attached to the Holy Spirit. When next you pray to God the father through our Lord Jesus Christ, apply these code names.

The Spirit of God (Genesis 1:2).

The Holy Spirit (Luke 11:13)

The Holy Spirit of Jehovah (Isaiah 61:1)

The Spirit (John 3:6)

The Spirit of The Lord (Isaiah 11:12)

The spirit of your father (Mathew 10:20)

The Spirit of the living God (2 Corinthians 3:3)

The spirit of Grace (Zechariah 12:10; Hebrew 10:29)

The spirit of Truth (John 14:17, 18; 15:26; 16:13)

The Spirit of Holiness (Romans 1:4)

The spirit of life (Roman 8:2)

The spirit of Christ (Roman 8:9)

The spirit of Adoption (Roman 8:15)

The spirit of His Son (Galatians 4:6)
The spirit of Glory (1 Peter 4:14)
The spirit of Prophesy (Revelation 19:10)
The Helper (John 14:16,26)
Eternal Spirit (Hebrew 9:14)
The spirit of Jesus Christ (Philippians 1:19 Acts 16:7)
The Spirit of Burning (Isaiah 4:4)
The spirit of promise (Ephesians 1:13)
The spirit of wisdom and understanding the spirit of counsel and might; the spirit of knowledge – these thoughts and names occur in (Isaiah 11:1-2).
The oil of gladness (Hebrew 1:9).
The Holy Spirit is also likened to a dove, which is both timid and gentle. He is likened to the wind (John 3:1-9) the unseen mysterious person behind regeneration is the Holy Spirit. He is like a spring of water, the cleaning force in sanctification (John 4:14). He is like an overflowing river of blessing in service, see John 7:38, 39. He is the comforter, consoling, guiding and directing the Christ life, John 14:16.

CHAPTER FOURTEEN
EFFECT/IMPACT OF THE HOLY SPIRIT

The dictionary meaning of effect is: the change that the first thing causes in the second thing". Example, parents worry about the effect of music, violent movies on their children's behavior. Head injuries can cause long lasting psychological effects.

The Holy Spirit, the third divine person of the Trinity raised Jesus Christ from the grave on the third day, and Jesus Christ in the same manner of impact of effect filled His followers with the promised Holy Spirit and He said that, the same Holy Spirit who had lived in Him would return to live in all those people who would open their hearts to His power. And they shall be empowered for service and they shall do greater things because of the Holy Spirit.

The last word Jesus proclaimed in Acts 1:8 was *"And ye shall receive power after the Holy Ghost is come upon you."* This is the power given to His church in witnessing, to impact lives through the proclamation of the Good News. The church of God needs to experience this miracle power of the Holy Spirit in healing, prophecy, love, faith, wisdom, divine health etc. since the gift is never limited to some few individuals, but for all who obediently open up their heart to receive, you therefore need to receive the Holy Spirit freely today!

During the revival conference that was organized by the Divine Light Ambassadors Church (DLA Church) (Ebenezer Chapel) Ekpoma Branch, theme: *"Healing Wings"* on May 24th-29th 2005, there was a great demonstration of the Holy Spirit through the hand of our Senior Pastor, Apostle Bernard Edehomon and the Holy Spirit joined the hearts of many people together in Christ and made them become members of one family of God under the auspices of Divine Light Family, the family of love.

That faithful day was like the day of Pentecost, many who heard Pastor Bernard Edehomo preach had their lives changed. Many asked to be baptized and the new members of the church spent their time learning in fellowship together, sharing in meals and worship. The Holy Spirit spoke through my Senior Pastor Bernard Edehomon, President/Head of Missions, and he declared God's word powerfully. As he stood preaching, a certain man rushed toward the platform (Alter) with his hands raised in surrender to God and I heard him creaming and crying, shouting the name of Jesus Christ. The man testified to the goodness of the Holy Spirit that, since he has been a Christian for the past 20 years, he has never in his lifetime received such an encounter with Jesus Christ. The Holy Spirit is a powerful personality who when he comes upon a person, he/she becomes speechless like Apostle

Paul at his conversion, on his way to Damascus, he met with Him and for a moment all his emotions dried up and he was purified.

Many sick persons who were in attendance at the *"Healing Wings" Revival Conference* received healing during that powerful sermon by Pastor Bernard Edehomon. They all testified to the goodness of the Holy Spirit on Sunday 29th May 2005, being the last of the conference, in the presence, of multitude of people. Epilepsy, paralysis, high blood pressure, barrenness, stroke and fear were all kicked out forever in the name of Jesus Christ.

In addition, at Lagos State Headquarter of Divine Light Ambassadors Church (Favor Chapel), one brother Joseph from the Western part of Nigeria was equally healed of HIV type 1 and 2, after Senior Pastor Bernard had prayed for him. He commanded him in the name of Jesus to go back for another test in the same hospital where he tested positive and he obeyed, behold he returned with another result proving he was now HIV negative. We should never underestimate the Holy Spirit powerful effect in ministry for healing and witnessing.

Apostle Paul in one of his letters to the Corinthians in Ephesus (a town in Asia Minor) declared the effect of the Holy Spirit, that we should be humble, gentle and patient, always showing our love in helping one another. Gentle, and patient, always showing our love in helping one another. This was why David Livingstone, a medical doctor, trained at the famous University of Glasgow became an evangelist and a soul winner. He used his knowledge of medical practice in conjunction with the power of the Holy Spirit to win many soils for Christ in Africa. Through the effect of the Holy Spirit, he travelled the length of Kalahari Desert, through the jungles of Angola Zambezi River and Victoria Falls.

Also, he gained the confidence of the natives not only by providing free medical services for the sick, but also he learned to speak their languages and prayed earnestly for their conversion.

CHAPTER FIFTEEN
THE HOLY SPIRIT AS COUNSELLOR

The word 'counselor' means one who gives advice and direction for life. *"But the Counselor, the Holy Spirit, whom the father will send in my name, will teach you all things and will remind you of everything I have said to you" (John 14:26) NIV).*

Human counselors are described in the Holy Scriptures as follows: human counselors (Isaiah 3:3) are described as, the captain of fifty and the honorable man, the counsels and the skillful artisan and the expert enchanter. Without counsel plans will fail (Proverb 22:20-21). *"Plan fails for lack of counsel but with advisers they succeed 15:22 (NIV).*

The wisdom of God gives us counsel (Psalm 119:24). David succeeded in his reign because he used counselor (1 Chronicles 27:32-33), he placed wise/good counselor around himself. These counselors always prayed to God for direction and his reign as king of Israel was successful. Jeremiah was a good counselor too (Jeremiah 38: 14-27).

Foolish counsel will always ruin a government or community and every wicked counselor must be rejected in any community, town or church (Job 21:16; Ps 1:1).

"The counsel of the wicked is far from me" Job 21:16b. Rehoboam followed foolish counselors as well as the Babylonians who had

poor counselors (1 King 12:1-16, Isaiah 47:13) and this led to their fall. *" All the counsel you have received has only worm you out! Let your astrologers come forward, those stargazers who make prediction month by month, let them save you from what is coming upon you "Isaiah 47:13 (NIV).*

The Almighty God is the true counselor (Psalm 116.7). *I will praise the LORD, who counsels me; even at night my heart instructs me"* (NIV).

\ God guides and leads us in His counsel of truth and Holiness (see Psalm 73:24; Isaiah 28:29). *You will guide me with your counsel and afterward receive me to glory"* Psalm 73:24. Jesus Christ is the counsel as prophesied by prophet Isaiah in Isaiah 9:6. "For to us a child is born to us a son is given, and the government will be on His shoulders. And he will be called wonderful Counselor, Mighty God, Everlasting Father, Prince of Peace" (NIV). The Holy Spirit of Christ is now counselor. "... *The Spirit of the LORD shall rest on Him, the spirit of wisdom and understanding the spirit of counsel and might..."* (Isaiah 11:1-2).

For scripture references (see John 14:16;26;15:26, 16:7)

CHAPTER SIXTEEN
THE HOLY SPIRIT AS A TEACHER

The Holy Spirit is a teacher who discloses all things hidden from the ordinary man. *"We have not received the spirit of the world but the spirit who is from God, that we may understand what God has freely given us. This is what we speak, not in words taught us by human wisdom but in words taught by the Spirit, expressing spiritual truths in spiritual words"*. (1 Corinthians 2:12, 13).

The spirit teaches things far from men (mysteries) and searches all things even the deep things of God. Only a spiritual man knows the thought of God and the power behind creation.

The Bible says in 1 Corinthian 2:7-8, that we speak of God's secret wisdom which is hidden from the rulers of this age (devil and his agents). *No eyes has seen, no ear has heard, nor mind has conceived what God has prepared for those who loved Him"* (1Corinthnians 2:9)

The Holy Spirit as a teacher, teaches us to know Christ better in His excellent wisdom and revelation. *"Do not cease to give thanks for you, making mention of you in my prayers: that the God of our Lord Jesus Christ, the father of glory, may give to you the Spirit of wisdom and revelation in the knowledge of Him"* (Ephesians 1:16, 17).

He reveals the things of God to His people. *"Who has understand the mind of the LORD, or instructed him as his counselor? whom did the*

Lord consult to enlighten him and who taught him the path of understanding" (Isaiah 40:13,14) NIV.

God reveals things to us by His Spirit, teaching us all the deep things of His Kingdom.

I was raised in an idolatrous home, where typical traditions and rituals are done. But by His special grace, the Lord separated me and choose me, delivered me and sent me to open the eyes of the blind, to turn them from darkness to light, and from the power of Satan to God, that they may receive forgiveness of sins and an inheritance among those who are sanctify by faith in Christ Jesus.

The Holy Spirit is the person that taught me the Holy Scripture to scripture. *"But the anointing which you have received from Him abides in you, and you do not need that anyone teach you; but as the same anointing teaches you concerning all things, and is true, and is not a lie and even as it has taught you, you will abide in Him" (1 John 2:27)*

The bible says in 1 Corinthians 2:11-13: for what man knows the things of man except the spirit of the man which is in Him? Even so no one knows the things of God except the Spirit of God. Now we have received not the spirit of the world, But the spirit of God. Now we have received, not the spirit of the world, But the spirit who is from God. These things we also speak, not in words which man's wisdom teaches but which the Holy

Spirit teaches, comparing spiritual things with the spiritual.

Even if you are in a seminary or theological institute, you need to be taught first by the Holy Spirit, otherwise all you efforts will be in vain! After I was taught by the Holy Spirit, I went for an online bible college in Australia, Virtue Campus for Biblical Studies, WBS (Word Bible School) USA, FULL GOSPEL BIBLE INSTITUTE,COATEVILLE, PENNESYLVANIA, U.S.A,. New Life Correspondence School NORWAY, and other leadership courses in Alpha course in the Church of Christ the King (Anglican Communion Tripoli, Libya), also as you are obedient in serving the church where there Lord placed you, you shall also be taught by Him often.

The Holy Spirit is the teacher, it was pointed out by Jesus Christ Himself in Luke 12:11-12. *"Now when they bring you to the Synagogues and magistrates and authorities do not worry about how or what you should answer, or what you should say. For the Holy Spirit will teach you in that very hour what you ought to say."*

Jesus Christ attended the Holy Ghost University, he is the best teacher. A human bible institute may deviate to teach human Doctrine Dogma, and Politics, but the Holy Spirit teaches mysteries, the way and never religion.

CHAPTER SEVENTEEN
THE HOLY SPIRIT AND INTERCESSION

To intercede means, "To strike upon, to appeal or to attack anyone with petitions on behalf of others."

In Hebrew it is offered as *"Paga" and it means, "to strike upon"* while in Greek the Word is offered as *"entugchanein"* and it means, "to appeal or petition". *Intercede" is a verb word used five times in the NT (New Testament). "And Festus said... King Agrippa and all the men who are here present with us, you see this man about whom the whole assembly of the Jews petitioned me both at Jerusalem and here, crying out that he was not fit to live any longer"* (Acts 25:24). Also see Romans 8:27, 34; Hebrews 7:25.

In other words, intercession is a prayer offered by one or more persons on behalf of another. In the Old testament, priest, prophets and kings usually did it. In the New Testament under the dispensation of grace, the Bible teaches that all churches and Christian leaders should embrace the responsibility of offcring prayers of intercessions for all men, kings and those in authority. The noun, intercession, occurs twice. *"Therefore, I exhort first of all that supplications, prayers, intercession, and giving of thanks be made for all men, for kings and all who are in authority that we may lead a quiet and peaceable life in all godliness and reverence"* (1 Timothy 2:1-2,4:5).

"For it is sanctified by the word of God and prayer". (1 Timothy 4:5)

We see that there is a contrast in the use of the word "intercession" in 1Timothy 2:1 with "supplications, prayers and giving thanks".

Trench defined "intercession" as, not only something satisfactorily rendered in prayer for others (1 Timothy 4:5), but a pleasing either for them or against them… as regards the Greek word *"entugchanein"*, appeal or petition through familiar speech in communing with God in prayer. To be able to intercede for others you need the natural/spiritual boldness and familiarity in prayers. Remember that through the power of the Holy Spirit who now dwells in us (believers) we have received boldness to approach His throne. *"Therefore, brethren having boldness to enter the Holiest by the blood of Jesus" (Hebrews 10:19).*

\ We see in the Bible, the patriarch, like Abraham, Esther and Church leaders like Paul and the elders, who were challenges to pray and intercede for others. Christ is our great intercessor, while on earth. He prayed and manifested God's glory for all to see; even now as He is at the right hand of the father. He is still praying to the father on our behalf. He brings our hurts, sorrows and weaknesses to the Father on our behalf. He brings makes intercession for us, because, we as human do not really know what we should pray for, especially in weakness and distress.

Apostle Paul said in 2 Corinthians 12:7-9 when he was attacked by Satan that, he requested and pleaded with the Lord three times to take away from him such deadly arrow, but the Lord always replied him saying: *My grace is sufficient for you, for my strength is made perfect in weakness". (2 Corinthians 12:9).*

So, never you give up, but remember always, that His grace is always available for you at the time of weakness. Jesus Christ never leaves us nor forsakes us, because His grace and His mercy are readily available for us abundantly. He is always ready to help the obedient children of God. *"Can a woman forget her nursing child and not have compassion on the son of her womb? Surely they may forget, yet I will not forget you"* (Isaiah 49:15)

"Be anxious for nothing, but in everything be prayer and supplication with thanksgiving let your request be made known to God" ***(Philippians 4:6).***

So, beloved go to God in prayer by intercession and choose some one in your family who has not yet given his/her life to Jesus Christ, even your community, people who still worship idols of any God, intercede on their behalf for deliverance.

<u>Biblical Intercessors:</u>

Abraham the father of faith intercede for the people of Sodom and Gomorrah in (Genesis 18:22-23).

Moses in the same manner prayed for the Israelites after they made the golden calf (Exodus 32:31-32).

Elijah, a man of prayer offered prayer of faith on Mount Carmel (1 King 18:36-37).

Esther declared a fast among the Jews in Shushan and made intercession, supplication and petition to save the Jews (Esther 4 and 5)

Which in the New Testament, our Lord Jesus Christ, the High Priest, always at the right hand of the Father in heaven, makes intercession for us.

" Who is he who condemn? It is Christ who died, and furthermore is also risen, who is even the right hand of God, who also makes intercession for us" (Romans 8:34).

"Therefore He is also able to save to the uttermost those who came to God through Him, since He always live to make intercession for them". (Hebrew 7:25).

The Ministry of Our Lord Jesus Christ has two aspects as follows:
He is our advocate
He is our intercessor
He pleads and makes petition to God when we sin against God., (see 1 John 2: 1-2) and He always keeps us from evil, *"I do not pray that you should*

take them out of the world, but that you should keep them from the evil one" (John 17:15).

Also see Luke 22:32; Jesus Christ prayed for Peter to stay in the faith, we should also pray for backsliding souls to enable them stay put in the faith.

The Book of Isaiah 53:1 says *for he bore sins of many and made intercession for the transgressors"*

We find access to God through Christ. (John 14:6)

The intercession of the Holy Spirit: The Holy Spirit intercedes on behalf of the believers with unutterable groaning. All times we pray and feel weak without hope, again immediately the Holy Spirit comes to renew our heart bringing hope, relief and encouragement of possibilities of anwers coming from God.

The Intercession of Christians: This is usually on behalf of all men, carried out by all believers especially the church leaders including Elders prayer interccdes for the well being of the nations, in order that they may have true knowledge of the truth of salvation in Christ and be saved (1 Timothy 2:1-4) well, all believers are priests and kings: in the Old Testament, the stiff necked Israelites asked for a king in error and sinned against God. Pray to the LORD your God for your servants so that we will not die, for we have address to all our other sins the evil of asking for king" (1 Samuel 12:19) NIV).

This was when the Israelites rejected their leader to seek for the tall handsome Saul who led them to doom. Many people today around the globe, especially Africa, are still suffering from their evil and greedy deeds in choosing the wrong leaders for selfish purpose and God permits us to make our choice, since we are created as free moral agents. There is no leadership on earth that God is not aware of, it is for us to learn a lesson and repent from our past mistakes and ask for prayer like the Israelites. Until we ask for prayer; the problem of poverty and corruption shall linger on, a prayer of intercession can be much effective when confession of sin is made already. This is why in every church service, we make prayers of confession, to be able to stand before His throne of grace, making intercession. Our prayers are not usually answered because of filthy sins (Isaiah 59:1-2)

"Righteousness exalts a nation but sin is a reproach to any people" Proverbs 14:34.

When I arrived Lagos-Nigeria in the month of December 2004, at the Murtala Mohammed Airport, God took me to the above scripture in Proverbs 14:34 and told me to intercede for Nigeria. He divinely instructed me to be going to secondary and tertiary institutions, hospital, businessmen and women, kings and those in political authority and prisons to preach and conduct intercessory prayers for the people. Brethren we need to persistently offer prayers for all and ourselves taught by our Lord Jesus Christ.

1 Chronicles 16:11 says, "Seek the LORD and His strength, seek His face continually".

Luke 18:1-7 reveals a widow's intercessory work, she kept crying to the Lord day and night and the Lord specially avenged her adversaries as she continually troubled the Lord in prayer (see also psalm 55:17).

The Holy Spirit makes us to pray according to the will of God and He gives us boldness against our enemies and their threats (Acts 4:28-31; 13:2-3). Samuel prayed in the power of the Holy Spirit at Mizpah and gained victory over the philistines) 1 Samuel 7:5-13).

CHAPTER EIGHTEEN
BEARING FRUIT FOR GOD

To be able to bear fruit for God, He encouraged his people in the O.T. (Old Testament) to meditate on Him, His law and his works with the mind we should focus our attention on God's reality and seek to develop a sense of his presence in order to grow in trust, reverence and joy.

The entire book of Psalms helps us to commune with God. Jesus Christ our Lord and personal savior regularly engaged in personal prayer and meditation as well as the early Christians of the early church and they produced fruit as a result of this exercise, through the power of the Holy Spirit. (Note Mathew 3:8-10).

Through personal quiet times with the lord in fasting and prayer and confession of our evil deeds, we cultivate a sense of peace in a world of unrest.

"… In returning and rest you shall be saved, in quietness and confidence shall be your strength (Isaiah 30:15) (Acts 3:19).

When we confess our sins, fast and pray and meditate on the word of the LORD, we develop a close relationship with God and bear fruit for the LORD Jesus Christ in building the Church. Fruit bearing enables us to make important decisions and obtain strength for Christian living and receive God's direction for our lives.

"You will know them by their fruits. Do men gather grapes from thorn bushes or figs from thistles? Even so, every good tree bears good fruit but a bad tree bears had fruit. A good tree cannot bear bad fruit nor can a bad tree bear good fruit. Every tree that does no bear good fruit is cut down and throw into the fire. Therefore, by their fruit you will known them (Mathew 7:16-20).

Florence Nightingale, Born 12th May 1820, at a city in Italy, died 1910. Until her death she produced fruit for the LORD and was best known for her diligence, dedication and nobility to the nursing profession. These two incidents in her life made her to be trained as a nurse. She was motivated to read Nursing because it hurt her to see young women dying without much help from anyone. She felt that if she had some medical knowledge, she could have made efforts by the power of the Holy Spirit to save the young women's lives. She often read the Lord's statement in Mathew which says, *"Verily I say unto you in as much as you have done it unto one of the least of those my brethren, ye have done it unto me"* (Mathew 25:40).

It is no secret what the Lord can do, if you will believe. The Lord uses men to accomplish His will through their task. D.L. Moody, born in Northfield, Massachusetts, USA on February 5, 1837, win more souls for the Lord than his temporaries through God's grace and the Holy

Spirit operation in His ministry moody produced fruit for the Lord in his time; recorded more than 750,000 established converts as a soul winner. He was a workaholic; this made many of his members to be up and doing. His impact was so much that one of his workers- Ira. D. Sankey, his chief choirmaster in the evangelistic outreaches and composer of many Christian hymns, was overheard praying:

"God make moody tired or give the rest of us his kind of super human strength" he founded the Moody Bible Institute and the Moody press. Moody died in 1988 at 62.

Also, John Bunyan, Born 1628, was by profession a thinker, he lived in England, he was a born again Christian who never compromised God's work he was tagged a non-conformist, he took the risk of imprisonment for preaching Christ (gospel) openly and was sent to jail by human judge. There in the jail he received the inspiration to write the Pilgrim's Progress right there in the cell, he dreamt about the born again Christian's journey from the city of Destruction to the Celestial City. Part 1 of it was published in 1684. Today, he is best known for his immortal literacy classics, the Pilgrim's Progress one of the best sellers in the world and has come to acquire a far-reaching appeal for people of every age. His intelligence and education has enabled him to spread the Good News of our Lord Jesus Christ.

William Booth, born April 10,1829   in Nottingham. England as a pawn-broker in his early ages came in contact with a teeming population of the under privileged: the poor the famished and the burdened and be became convinced that spiritual poverty was the cause of people's wretchedness, misfortunes and misery. This conviction came to him after his conversion and the Lord led him to launch the salvation army movement with his wife Catherine Booth, aimed at reaching the poor with the gospel.

William Booth was the first preacher in history to introduce the alter call practice in ministry. He never believed that a mere profession of conversion was sufficient to get a man saved. He made a global impact and won hundred of thousand of souls with the gospel during his lifetime, and slept in the LORD August, 20, 1912 at the age of 83. As a matter of fact, this is the vision of our Lord Jesus Christ, to preach the Good News to the uttermost part of the earth as part of fruit bearing (Mathew 24: 14). As a born again Christian and pastor/evangelist what vision do you have in realizing the great commission? I mean taking the gospel to your community, the people you relate with each day, you gospel to you community, the people you relate with each day, your neighbours and the rest part of the world?.

Martin Luther was a man like you, a former lecturer in moral philosophy at the University of

Wittenberg, born in Germany on November 11, 1483 ordained priest in 1505. He was a religious reformist during his lifetime. Prior to his conversion, he had believed his Church's theological dogma, which upheld penance and religious indulgences as the only way to salvation and forgiveness of sin. This was more different for him to obtain forgiveness and peace that the Lord gives to those who trust in His atoning forgiveness of sins.

By the special of grace of God, Luther was led by the Holy Spirit to embrace the plain truth of the scriptures that says, "the just shall live by faith" (Roman 1:17) and he also widely disseminated this Good News to far- reaching religious groups before his death on February 18, 1546.

Brothers and sisters, when will it be your turn? Why are you still bound to religious philosophies and legalism, dogmatism, doctrine of men, church politics and traditions of men? You need to discover the truth and bear good fruit. You need to preach the Kingdom of God and salvation to all mankind as in Acts 4:12. Do not remain bound to religious and mosaic laws that kill, but follow Christ; he is the one who gives us grace to live

CHAPTER NINETEEN
SYMBOLS/EMBLEMS OF THE HOLY SPIRIT

EMBLEMS OF THE HOLY SPIRIT

Water: (John 3:5, John 7:38, 39). Water is cleansing agent that helps to remove dirt. Jesus said in John 3:5"… verily, verily, I say to you, except a man be born of water and of the spirit he cannot enter into the kingdom of God".

Water is used figuratively in the following

Salvation of the spirit (John 4;14, Isaiah 12:3)

Baptism and of cleansing by the word of God (John 7:37-39, 15:3; Ephesians 5:25.

We are cleansed and born again by the word (James 1:18; 1 peter 1:23) it is clear that being born of water means, being born again by the word of God.

Water does five things in relationship to the spirit.

Water is freely given – Isaiah 55:1 John 4:14 revelation 22:17

Water fertilizers- the spirit filled Christians are like watered trees, psalm 1:3.

Water is abundant John 7:37 like over flowing rivers.

Water refreshes – John 4:4`4, Psalm 46: 4; Isaiah 41:12, 12, 18. Like the deer get refreshed by water in the brooks.

Water cleanses. Ephesians 5:26 the church was held and sanctified by the sprit and the word. This is a fundamental law in both natural and spiritual realms, that is, we live after the flesh or after the spirit (Roman 8:1-13; Galatians 5:16-26).

Like the natural man hears the wind blowing so the man born again hears the voice of the spirit.

Nicodemus because he operated in the flesh he could not easily discern the scripture as in Jeremiah 31:33; 32:39 and Jesus expected him to know the scriptures enough to be saved; but he was like many in the church today, even among ministers of the Gospel, who lack the proper understanding of the new birth. Nicodemus though he spent most of his life in his unbelief (doubt) about spiritual matters, latter accepted the truth (John 19:39). This is my prayer for a lot of most pastors in Jesus name.

Wind: Which is spoken of in John 3:8 is also an emblem of the Holy Spirit.

    a. **Cannot** be seen but very effective-John 3:8 like the spirit works in man.

    b. Wind is independent-John 3:8, 1Corinthians 12:17. The Holy Spirit is sovereign, acting in unity with the father and son.

    c. Wind is powerful- Luke 19:11, Acts 2:2. His power is unsearchable, mighty in creation.

d. Wind is reviving- Ezekiel 37:9, 10, 14. The Spirit (wind) revives the dead bodies.

Fire: Mathew 3:11 *"... he shall baptize you with the Holy Spirit and with fire.*

(a) Fire illuminates – John 5:35, John the Baptist, full of the Holy Spirit shone as a burning light.

(b) Fire burns-John- John 5:35 The spirit of burning burned in John the Baptist, see Isaiah 4:4.

(c) Fire purifies, Malachi 3:2,3 The Holy Spirit is like a refining fire that purifies and brings to perfection.

(d) Fire searches, The Holy Spirit, like fire cannot be stationed, but searches all things. Yes, the deep things of God 1 Corinthians 2:10.

Oil: Psalm 45:7 *"... anointed thee with the oil of gladness above thy fellows.*

(a) Oil consecrates – Oil in O.T. (Old Testament) was used for consecration, Exodus 29:7 also see Luke 4:18

(b) Oil illuminates, Mathew 25, the foolish virgins without oil couldn't shine.

(c) Oil comforts- Isaiah 61:3 *"... the oil of joy for mourning"* See Hebrews 1:9.

Dove: Mathew 3:16 The Spirit as a dove on Jesus during baptism in Jordan.

(a) The dove is very gentle Mathew 10:16 *"Harmless as doves…"* fruit of gentleness, Galatians 5:22

Rain and dew: Psalm 72.6 *"He shall come down like rain upon the mown grass.*

(a) Rain is very small like the seed of plant, Mark 4:26-29

(b) Rain refreshes, psalm 68:9; Isaiah 18:4

(c) Rain is abundant – Psalm 133:3, it is countless: no one can measure the dew, rain or the spirit.

(d) Rain fertilizers- Ezekiel 34:26, 27, The Showers of blessing can cause the tiniest to germinate and grow.

Voice: Isaiah 6:8 "… The Voice of the Lord Saying …"

(a)The voice guides- Isaiah 30:21 the spirit's voice guides us into truth see John 16:13.

(b) The voice speaks Mathew 10:20 *"…. The spirit of your father which Speaketh in you"*

(c) The voice warns- Hebrews 3:7-11, John 16:7-11 warming of sin, righteousness and judgment.

Seal: The Holy Spirit is like a seal of agreement as a sign of ownership "… whereby you are sealed unto the day of redemption". Revelation 7:2 Ephesians

4:30. The Holy Spirit is Himself the seal, in the symbolism of scriptures. A seal signifies a concluded transaction, Jeremiah 32:9, 10.   Ownership, Jeremiah 30:1, 11,12; 2 Timothy 2:19 security, Esther 5:8; Daniel 1:7 Ephesians 4:30

(a) A seal authenticates (John 6:27; 2 Corinthians 1:22). Believers are marked and branded by the Spirit.

"... For I bear in my body the marks of the Lord Jesus" (Galatians 6:17).

I remember when I was a child, my mother then was a rice dealer and on every of her goods was written with ink J.E. Symbolizing that she is the owner, this secured the goods for her until the final transaction was made.

(b) A seal secures –Ephesians 1:13 14, this is the down payment which secures the transaction of a deal (showing a sign of Christ's purchase on the cross of calvary).

The Christian life is lived in the spirit and power of the Holy Spirit which teaches us all things by the Anointing of the Holy Spirit for understanding of God's truth.

This anointing comes after the fire of the Holy Spirit and righteousness of Christ, burn wickedness out of our Lives and

He empowers us for service. There is only one anointing (see Acts 1:8, 2 Corinthians 1:21, 22: 1 John 2:20, Acts 4:31) and this anointing of the spirit received by faith (John 7:37-39; John 4:14).

Our Lord Jesus Christ was sealed during His baptism in River Jordan (See Ephesians 1:13, 17;2:18, 23; Mathew 1:18; Acts 2:4)

You can partner with our evangelistic Outreach and help us spread the Gospel as follows:

Tick as appropriate
□ Crusade/ Mission □ DOERS WORD OUTREACH partnership □ Special offering for □ TV Ministry/ Radio Ministry

Orphans and widows in affliction
Building □ Seed offering for mission trip overseas □ Other (specify) □ Book publishing

"Give and it will be given to you. A good measure pressed down shaken together and running over, will be poured into your bosom for the measure you use, it will be measured to you" (Luke. 6:38)

<u>**Banking Details**</u>

Bank Name: Wells Fargo
Account Number: 1843761105
Account Name: Jacob I. Edehomo
Routing Number (RTN) 021200025
Postal Address: 820 Grove street, Irvington, NJ,07111-3674, USA.

Mobile/ SMS Line
+1717-329-6321

Please if you have completed this partnership forms and paid to the Bank, indicate by sending us SMS with above mobile phone numbers or send us email to eromodion1@yahoo.co.uk

We would love to hear from you. May the Good Lord bless you in Jesus Name,Amen.